PROSPERO'S SON

PROSPERO'S SON

Life, Books, Love, and Theater

Seth Lerer

THE UNIVERSITY OF CHICAGO PRESS * *Chicago & London*

SETH LERER is dean of arts and humanities at the University of
California, San Diego. He is the author of many books, including the
National Book Critics Circle Award–winning *Children's Literature:
A Reader's History, from Aesop to Harry Potter*, also published by the
University of Chicago Press.

The University of Chicago Press, Chicago 60637
The University of Chicago Press, Ltd., London
© 2013 by The University of Chicago
All rights reserved. Published 2013.
Printed in the United States of America
22 21 20 19 18 17 16 15 14 13   1 2 3 4 5

ISBN-13: 978-0-226-01441-8 (cloth)
ISBN-13: 978-0-226-01455-5 (e-book)

Library of Congress Cataloging-in-Publication Data

Lerer, Seth, 1955–
    Prospero's son : life, books, love, and theater / Seth Lerer.
    pages. cm.
    ISBN 978-0-226-01441-8 (cloth : alk. paper)
    ISBN 978-0-226-01455-5 (e-book)
    1. Lerer, Seth, 1955– —Family.   2. English teachers—United States—
Biography.   I. Title.
PR55.L47A3 2013
801'.95092—dc23
[B]

                                                          2012045004

⊚ This paper meets the requirements of ANSI/
NISO Z39.48-1992 (Permanence of Paper).

CONTENTS

First Love

The autumn I turned fourteen, I came down with whooping cough. Like everybody of my generation, I was vaccinated as a child, and by the late 1960s incidences of the illness had been reduced to one in a hundred thousand. But as ninth grade began, I found myself uncontrollably wheezing after what seemed like a mild cold. Half a dozen deep coughs would come, followed by a grip across my chest that stopped my breathing. I'd stand up, gasping for breath, the air coming in through my tightened throat with a high-pitched whoop. And then I breathed again.

It's not as if I'd been a sickly child: no chronic illnesses, no months in bed, no frail, fantasy-ridden birthdays. All I remember is that from about the age of six till the time I was twelve, I always had a cold. Days would go by when I would sniffle, blow, and watch packs of handkerchiefs fill with sticky green snot. "If you sniffle one more time I'll cut your nose off," I remember my father blurting out once in the car. When I was seven, I was taken to a doctor who drained my sinuses with a pneumatic syringe, and I sat in his office chair, watching a glass jar fill with bubbling mucus. I read and sniffled my way into adolescence. Propped up in bed, I'd reach for a tissue as often as I'd turn a page. Finally, at twelve, I had my adenoids removed, an awful hospital procedure that left me bleeding from the throat for days and eating only Jell-O for a week. One day after my operation, when we were in a store, I coughed up some blood. A blob of dark, congealing goo stared up from the store's carpet, and as we hustled out the door my mother said, "Well, that's the last time I can go to Loehmann's."

Mom took her anger out on me, but she may have been angrier with my father. Just a year before, he had uprooted us to follow his ambition. Some men dream of being firemen or doctors or air aces. My Dad dreamed of being a high school principal. A dozen years of New York City classroom history teaching and low-level junior high administration weren't paying off, and so at thirty-nine he had applied and, miraculously, been accepted into Harvard's Graduate School of Education. Now, he could be "Dr. Lerer" and lead one of the great high schools that made Brooklyn famous: Midwood, or even Erasmus.

In 1965, when I was ten, we moved from Brooklyn into a little house near Cambridge, where I grew strawberries in the backyard and read science fiction in my room. The first day of school, Dad was sent home because he wore a sports shirt to class. "Mr. Lerer, all my students wear jackets and ties," he reported his professor saying. The Harvard Club was serving horse meat in mushroom sauce on Fridays. Radcliffe girls wore tartan skirts with their hair in buns. And I was reading Aldous Huxley's *Brave New World*, Yevgeny Zamyatin's *We*, and George Orwell's *1984*, imagining myself a hero in the future, with clean sinuses, while Dad went out and bought a dozen white shirts and a clutch of skinny dark ties. He smoked, I sniffled, and I watched him read and study all the books that would define the social science of the 1960s: Daniel Moynihan and Gunnar Myrdal on race, Staughton Lynd on class. I scanned his bookshelf: H. R. Hays, *From Ape to Angel*; Edgar Friedenberg, *The Dignity of Youth and Other Atavisms*. I had no idea what an atavism was, but I knew I had little dignity. And though I never dared open *From Ape to Angel*, I imagined it a book of evolutionary science fiction on a par with Huxley—creatures captured by ambitious scientists, placed in some marvelous machine, and transformed into ethereal beauties.

Two years later, despite his Harvard EdD, Dad had still not been transformed from ape to angel. There we were at graduation, with the mayor coming in on horseback and everyone in caps and gowns, looking like characters out of a medieval missal. Commencement 1967: Leonard Bernstein and William F. Buckley received honorary doctorates; ancient alumni strode by with straw boaters, each festooned with a crimson ribbon giving the wearer's class year. One such alumnus, nearly blind, came up to Dad after the ceremony and said, "Excuse me, young man, but can you tell me how to get to Adams House, where I used to take my meals." He had 1887 on his ribbon.

That day I decided I would spend my life in college. I read everything I could that summer, opened and closed the local public library, started the new school year charged with a desire to excel. But no white shirts could change my Dad, and eighteen months after receiving his degree, he came home to announce that we were moving. No school would have him as a principal, no system as a superintendent. Desperate, he had taken a job as a management consultant in Pittsburgh at a firm that, he told us years later, then existed only in the briefcase of the man who interviewed him. He had bought a seven-bedroom stone house in the suburbs, and we were all going to drive there after Christmas. Almost overnight, we disappeared—everything packed, the house sold, friends gone. It was as if we had entered the witness protection program. All I managed to keep were my books and a pair of paisley hip-hugger bell-bottoms I'd bought at Truc on Brattle Street—a shop that opened shortly after *Yellow Submarine* debuted at the movies.

And so, in the fall of ninth grade, when my nose and throat flared up, it was the big stone house in Pittsburgh that rattled with my whooping. I missed forty days of school. Friends would bring homework over to the house, and I would dutifully keep up with classes, anxious to return. There was a group of three or four girls whom I liked, and before I got sick we would spend our afternoons in the school library, flirting and talking about books, friends, and teachers. During my time at home, one or more of them would show up with the assignments and papers, coyly chatting with my mother at the door, never daring to come into the house and see how I was doing.

One day, I got a stack of readings from one of those girls. Her name was Anne, and she had brilliant red hair, which she kept in place with an Indian headband. With that, her granny glasses, and her boots, she looked like a sweeter version of the girl with Richard Brautigan on the cover of his novel *Trout Fishing in America*, which we all were reading at the time.

Anne left a stack of books along with copies of the student newspaper, and I went downstairs, after she had left, to pick them up. As I read through the newspapers, I noticed that along the margins, between the lines, and in the large indents for paragraphs, Anne had written, in a tiny, mechanical-penciled hand, "I love you."

I love you was everywhere. It filled the pages up and down until hardly a white space was visible. I sat there in bed, poring over her scribbles, again and again. Just seeing those words had a magical, incantatory effect. Reading them over and over was like a talking cure, a formula, as if she were truly wishing me well.

It's hard to remember a time before cell phones, e-mail, and text messaging. We had one phone in the house, and it would never have occurred to me to come downstairs and call her, even if I had had her number. What if her parents answered? What if my parents heard me calling? Instead, I pulled the big white pages out of the closet, found her last name in a column of adults, initials, and numbers, and tore it out. At night, I'd pull the page out from under the mattress, where I hid it, and just read down the initials and the numbers, trying to imagine which one she belonged to, where she lived, and what her parents did.

Weeks later, when I was better, I returned to school, and on an early afternoon in November I found her waiting for the bus. I got on with her and we talked all the way to her stop, where she got out and walked home, and I stayed on until the bus made its entire loop and took me back to school, where I got out and then walked home, an hour late for dinner.

We soon became inseparable. We held hands in the cafeteria, walked to classes, kissed in stairwells. I finally went over to her house to meet her parents, a dour couple, older than my own. Her father worked for US Steel and wore rimless glasses and a dark green hat. Sitting in their living room, still in his suit jacket from the day's work, he looked like John Foster Dulles, presiding over some domestic détente, a relic of the Eisenhower years trapped in the autumn of *Abbey Road.* My only memory of her mother is of the time she turned to me, almost out of nowhere, repeated my name twice, as if it were a Martian's, and said, "What kind of name is that?"

Anne made me chocolate cakes in her mother's kitchen. She knitted me scarves and gloves. Some afternoons, we sat together on the couch, an afghan covering us, while her father read aloud from *The Education of Henry Adams,* and she touched my crotch. Some nights, I'd stay for dinner, and we'd watch the war on television, her father silently fuming. I knew better than to say anything, having already been sent home once from school for wearing a black armband in protest (I was sent home two other times: once, for wearing my Cambridge bell-bottoms, deemed inappropriate attire by the homeroom teacher; the other time, for bringing a copy of *Portnoy's Complaint* to read in study hall). I passed the fall of 1969 at another family's dinner table, letting my hair grow to my collar, watching Walter Cronkite and listening to Henry Adams.

By March, Henry Adams had left for England with his father. Prince Sihanouk had been deposed in a Cambodian coup. My hair grew as long as Anne's. And when I showed up after school one day, there was her older sister, sitting at the piano, playing Bach's Prelude in D Major from the first book of *The Well-Tempered Clavier*, and smoking a cigarette. I didn't even know there *was* a sister. Twenty, tall, she was as strikingly beautiful as Anne was sweetly plain. The house was electric with anger, John Foster Dulles on the phone, talking as if he were renegotiating the Suez treaty. Sister was back, dropped out of college, ready to marry her boyfriend and expecting the family to cover it.

The wedding was in April, and for the occasion I went out and bought a blue blazer with lapels wide as 1950s car fins, red-and-white-striped bell-bottoms, and a blue knit tie so fat I hardly had to worry about buttoning my shirt. The groom showed up with blond hair down his back and a collection of college buddies strangely reticent to mingle. His own parents were Ohio people—"We're Ohio people," they said, in a way that was supposed to sound meaningfully self-explanatory, like saying, "We're vegetarians." The hippies and the homespun mingled in the Methodist church, and Anne's father gave her sister away with a look on his face like he was passing a stone.

I was the youngest person there, and as I sat in the pew with Anne all I could think of was her father reading Henry Adams. "As far as outward bearing went," wrote Adams in an early chapter, "such a family of turbulent children, given free rein by their parents, or indifferent to check, should have come to more or less grief." Anne's father must have read these words, must have recited them to us, convinced that, in the end, his own would grow up much like Henry's family, "to be decent citizens."

But they did not. The sister and her husband were escaping to Canada, his ushers standing at the ready to drive them all night along the highway to the border. He was avoiding the draft. She was three months pregnant. But at the wedding, we all danced to *Let It Be* on the hi-fi, hugged during "Two of Us," kissed during "Across the Universe." I looked at Anne, listening to the words "nothing's gonna change my world," and thought that everything would stay just like it was. And then, when "The Long and Winding Road" came on, I could see in her sister's eyes a sadness of such depth as I'd never seen in anyone. "The profoundest lessons," Henry Adams wrote, "are not the lessons of reason; they are sudden strains that permanently warp the mind."

That night, we sat on the unswept rice. Sister and new husband were gone; parents had returned home. We looked up at the stars and I saw them all as messages in bottles, washing up on our illicit shore. Anne took my hand and whispered in my ear, although no one else was there.

"I know what to do, now. She told me all about it, told me it would be fine."

"Told you what?"

"You know," Anne said, splaying her fingers on my lap.

Two days later, we went out to an open field after school. Even though it was May, the ground was still stubbly with the broken stalks of last fall's grasses, and the new growth hadn't come up far enough to soften the ground. She brought a blanket, and we made our bed over the stubble, lying side by side for nearly half an hour before we touched. Her eyes were closed the whole time, and I looked at her red hair as it crinkled and crept into the grasses by the blanket's edge. I touched her, and before I could turn that touch to a caress, she had her jeans off and her arms around me, pushing me into her. Everything then came off, I found her, and almost before we started it was over.

I looked down and we both were covered in blood. At first I thought it was mine, but then I realized that maybe this is what happened to a girl the first time. Then I realized that my mother would see blood on my underwear when she washed it. What was it, what had happened? She would sit me down under the kitchen lights like a prisoner of war and grill me till I broke. She'd beat her open palm against her forehead, as if I had violated *her*.

Anne shook me out of this rictus of remorse, bunched up my underwear, cleaned all of the blood off my legs, then hers, and threw the evidence into a ditch.

"Just go home in your jeans, walk in like nothing happened, and, if it's that important to you, get another pair of underwear on as soon as you can."

By this point, I was running only on my autonomic nervous system. Henry Adams and the Beatles had passed far out of my mind, and I was living in *Portnoy's Complaint*. All the titillations of Philip Roth's book had now morphed into terror. "Tell me please," I heard my mother saying, just like Alex Portnoy's, "what horrible things we have done to you all our lives that this should be our reward?" It's nothing, Mom. Just a little blood. "Nothing? Nothing?" she would repeat over and over again, and I sat there in the grass imagining her fit and remembering how I had coughed up blood at Loehmann's. And then, before I knew it, I was back home sitting in my dirty jeans at the dinner table, eating iceberg lettuce with Green Goddess dressing.

A week or so later, my parents announced that the whole family, including my eleven-year-old brother, was going to Europe for the summer. Dad had a friend when he was teaching in New York who had a ritual when he returned from vacation. "What did you see?" you were supposed to ask, and he would say, "Everything." "How did you go?" And he would pronounce, "First class." We flew to Paris, coach, from New York and arrived after midnight, Paris time. My mother had a little high school French, and when we got into the taxi at the airport, she announced the address of our hotel in a perfect, high school accent: *soixante-huit Rue des Martyrs*. The cabbie turned around and looked this middle-class American family up and down in disbelief. Thinking she had not said the address correctly, she gave him the letter from the Pittsburgh travel agent who had arranged our hotel stay. He shrugged his shoulders and drove us on.

Our hotel was just off the Place Pigalle, the heart of the hooker district. Even in 1970, there were prostitutes everywhere. Rouged and high-heeled, they patrolled the streets as if they had just reclaimed Paris from the German occupation. We lugged our bags up to the room and, without unpacking, fell asleep.

"The world," wrote Henry Adams, "contains no other spot than Paris where education can be pursued from every side." Would I be farmed out to a hooker, returning home to Anne with newfound skills? I couldn't get her father's voice out of my ears. It drowned out the street sounds, and I fell asleep hearing his drone. "The amusements of youth had to be abandoned," he would read, transforming Adams's easy irony into an injunction. But even the half-dream of Henry Adams couldn't keep me from the hotel window when a violent crash pulled us from sleep. I saw two cars, crumpled like concertinas, their windshields splattered across their hoods, and the two drivers, seemingly unhurt, screaming at each other. They yelled in something far beyond my mother's high school French for almost half an hour. Then, anger spent, they climbed back into their cars and drove away, each crumpled chassis creaking back and forth like a circus prop.

We woke up the next morning to the chatter of the prostitutes, their makeup smeared, their costumes disarrayed, their work done. The hotel's breakfast nook was cleared for the Americans, and my father's daylight face showed just how far from first class we were, fooled by the naïveté of our Pittsburgh travel agent ("quaint hotel in the heart of old Paris"). Mom and Dad acted out their anger. "How could you?" she accused. And him: "You're just upset because you're getting your period." "That's it! We're going to Fouquet's." In defiance, Mom announced that we were going to have lunch at the most famous restaurant she could recall, Fouquet's on the Champs-Élysées. She must have read about it as a teenager, the haunt of Chaplin, Chevalier, and Dietrich; a Brooklyn girl's fantasy of where the elite meet to eat.

We were not disappointed. Greeted at the door with graciousness and care by a mâitre d' with fluent English, the four of us, without a reservation, were escorted to a lovely table in the sun, handed a handwritten menu (which we could not read), and asked what kind of food we liked. "Roast beef," I said, and he replied, "That's fine, but I must warn you, it will be very rare." I acceded. It came, a slab cut from the whole roast, thick and bloody, practically quivering. I don't remember what anyone else had, but when the time came for dessert, Mom confessed to the mâitre d' that she had read a story once in which someone had eaten nothing but a perfect peach. He bowed slightly, snapped his fingers, and a young waiter in red came by. Words were exchanged, and, like a magician pulling something from a sleeve, he produced the largest, most fragrant, most perfect peach that any of us had ever seen.

Two subwaiters arrived. Mom was presented with a clean white plate, a little knife and fork, and a small glass of sweet white wine. The waiter took the peach, gauging its heft in his hand, and then took the back of a butter knife and deftly rubbed it all along the skin. Then, taking a tiny sharp knife, he made a small incision in the cleft. Setting the peach on the plate, cut side down, he placed his fingers around the top, squeezed a little, and the entire skin came off at once, revealing a whole, wet, blushing fruit. Mom clapped her hands together like a nine-year-old. And at that moment I knew that this mâitre d' knew more about my mother than we ever could: that what she wanted was a taste of magic; that all fruit, of whatever kind, should be presented as if it were sheathed in sin. And for those fifteen minutes that she ate that peach, I loved her.

We returned three weeks later to a Pittsburgh wreathed in summer smoke blown over from the mills along the river. Anne would not see me, would not answer the phone. I went over to her house to see if she was through with me, to see if all she'd wanted in that field was her adulthood. I knocked and found the door opened by her mother who looked at me as if I were a ghost. "She's not here." Who was the ghost now? When sophomore year began, I heard that she had run away, rumored to have become pregnant. Not by me, I was sure, though it was not until my senior year that I dared sleep with anyone again.

For forty years, I dreamed of her. I dreamed of her in college, when failed dates left me at the movies, and I wondered where she was. I dreamed of her after my parents divorced in the late seventies and left Pittsburgh forever—Mom returning to New York, Dad moving to DC—and I realized that I'd never see her again. I dreamed of her throughout the 1980s in Princeton, where I taught, and where I'd see her red hair in the autumn stubble. I dreamed of her after I moved to California with my wife in 1990, when my college students decided to stage a sixties party and asked me for fashion advice. They stood there in my Stanford office, well-cared-for children of the Reagan years, who knew no social trauma other than the *Challenger* disaster, dressed in macramé vests, beaded headbands, and paisley bell-bottoms.

I dreamed of her again, three years ago, the night after I saw my own son, at seventeen, and his girlfriend taking shelter at the laptop in his room. Nights once spent with his hobbies began to pass at the screen. Even when together, he and his girlfriend seemed to text rather than talk. There were no student newspapers to annotate, no notes to pass in class. Desire passed across touch pads, "I love you" evanescing in a keystroke. Will he have relics of his love? I still have bits and pieces of my high school life: a Pittsburgh bus transfer slipped as a bookmark in a novel; a letter written on the flyleaf of a Signet Shakespeare; a Polaroid faded to coppery sheen. One evening my wife and I came home to find him texting on the couch, two dirty dinner plates, two half-filled glasses, and two crumpled napkins on the dining table. He looked at me as if to say, "Don't tell Mom that I had a girl over." I quickly cleared the table, put the dishes in the dishwasher and turned it on, letting the rushing of its spray drown out the noise of our complicity, not letting on to Mom that there was anything amiss. That night, I would stay up until the cycle finished, to restore the clean, warm plates to cupboard stacks, without a trace of her.

ONE

Rough Magic

November 2003.

I was teaching *The Tempest* when the department office manager called me out of class. My comparative literature senior
seminar had eight students, all but one of them young women
whose fathers were college professors, social activists, artists, or
scientists. It was supposed to be a course in literary theory with
an emphasis on gender and interpretation, but the syllabus—
Shakespeare, Marx, Freud, Saussure, De Man, Erich Auerbach,
and Judith Butler—soon morphed into weekly meditations on
authority and pedagogy, reading things for what they weren't,
and the students' own literary tastes. Theory became a family
romance for them, a way of understanding authorship as if it were
paternalism, reading as if it were a household chore. We were a
few weeks into the seminar, finishing Shakespeare and turning to
later versions of the play—the postcolonial *Une Tempête* of Aimé
Césaire, the science fiction of *Forbidden Planet*—when the office
manager opened the door. "You have to come right now." I stared
across the table at my eager Mirandas and said, quietly, "I think
we'll have to stop."

I took the call in the department office, and before I even heard
the doctor's voice I knew that Dad was gone. I called my wife,

walked to my car without my coat in the rain, and drove to the hospital.

Driving.

As a child I never slept. At night, Dad would pile me into the car (no baby seat, no seat belts, a cigarette held out the window) and drive for hours till I dropped off. Sometimes, he would sing as he drove, his tuneless voice repeating the same nursery rhyme over and over.

> I had a little nut tree, nothing would it bear,
> But a silver nutmeg, and a golden pear.

And then I would awake in my own bed, not knowing how I got there, the smell of Kents hanging on my pj's like a caul.

Some nights, we'd all go out—Dad, Mom, my baby brother— just to fill the time. Whenever we got out of the car, my eyes would dart right to the ground. I'd pick up anything: a rusted bolt, a spent flashbulb, string, wire, pennies. I was collecting material for some great project, a machine that would transmute these scraps into a mystery, or that would reanimate the tossed-off body parts of old equipment. Every now and then, there'd be a real find. Once, when I was six, we drove out to Long Island to an Alexander's store to buy my mom a fur coat. In the parking lot, I found a piece of jetsam from another car. It may have been a solenoid, or a carburetor valve, or a gear. Whatever it had once been, it turned into a talisman in my pocket, and I held on to it on the ride back, as I fell asleep against Mom's new mouton coat.

And then, after we moved to Boston, there were the endless drives returning to New York to see relatives or friends. We always drove at night. Eight p.m. and the dinner dishes done, my father would announce, "Well, I don't know about you, but I'm ready to go." And sure as simpletons, my brother and I would jump up. Sure, let's go, what an adventure. Let's drive all night back to New

York. In those days, the two-hundred-and-forty-mile trip took nine hours, over old US highways, turnpikes, and toll roads. Stops along the way, great empty cities like Hartford, trucks, backups, midnight snacks. Then the wall of traffic when we reached Co-op City. Finally, the place we'd stay. "You're father was too cheap," Mom would say, "to spend a night in a real hotel. We always lived on handouts." But that was the way then. You were expected to drop in, you expected people. Anyone could come at any time. Keep the fridge full, you never know when guests might show up. When we moved to Boston, we kept the fridge full for three years. No one came.

One day, when I was in eleventh grade, my friends and I drove to Kentucky from Pittsburgh. It was one of those vague Saturdays of late high school, one of those I-don't-know-what-do-you-want-to-do days, and we piled into our old Renault and drove. Just drove. South, through Pennsylvania coal country, West Virginia hills. Cars up on blocks in gas stations for sale for seventy-five dollars, farm eggs a nickel apiece. We stopped at a roadside place where my friend, to my horror, ordered a liverwurst sandwich, and I don't know what I had but I pulled a twenty out of my wallet and the counter fell silent, like they'd never seen one before, and who was this kid with the Pennsylvania plates coming in with his buds and a twenty.

But that's what I learned from Dad: to pull a twenty from your wallet like it's magic, to show up out of nowhere and amaze the crowd and disappear.

Years later, I was listening to an interview with Shari Lewis on the radio, and she went on, not about Lamb Chop or her bangs, but about her dad. He was a founding member of Yeshiva University, and in the evenings after classes he would teach her magic tricks. "My father," she reflected, "was like the official magician of New York." Passing a closet one day, "Daddy heard my sister screaming to be let out. He opened the door, and my sister was nowhere to be seen." Shari had discovered her ability to throw her voice. Her parents put her onstage at eighteen months. "My parents were school teachers. They ran summer camps, and I was put onstage with a crepe-paper bow."

My father was the unofficial magician of New York. He did no juggling, no ventriloquism. Unlike my friends' fathers, he could not fix a leak, start a lawn mower, or change a broken lightbulb with a raw potato. He worked, instead, his magic in the car. The theater of his majesty was the front seat, as he drove almost without looking, talking to me next to him, waving at strangers out the window. I swear he had a third eye in his left ear; otherwise, how could he see the road?

We would drive for hours around Brooklyn, often with one of his friends (usually a former student who, now in his twenties, had little to do but cruise the city with a teacher and his kid), down Pitkin Avenue to Jacks, looking for two-dollar sport coats, or to the Knox Hat Shop, where rows of dark felt hats lay like corpses. I never remember my father wearing a hat, though. It was all part of his magic: the pompadoured hair, the high forehead. He didn't need a hat to pull anything out of. Some days we would walk into a restaurant, and people would turn, as if they'd expected us. We'd enter elevators, he would count to three and snap his fingers, and the doors would close. How did he do it? One night, when I was seven, we drove deep into Manhattan, parked, and came upon the Union Carbide Building. Inside, there was an exhibit about atoms, chemistry, and power. A model of a uranium atom spun inside a great blue plastic globe. It was like being taken on a tour of matter's very heart, and I held his hand as if he were my Christmas ghost flying me over unexpected streets.

I grew up longing to relive his skill. Once at a conference in the 1980s, I turned the corner of a book exhibit with two graduate students in tow, only to find a champagne reception in progress for a newly minted author. We were all handed glasses as if we had been expected, and I turned to my students and smiled. "Like how I did that?" There was the time, when I was teaching a freshman seminar at Stanford, that I trooped the students into downtown Palo Alto for a final lunch, and before we could hit the restaurant, we were accosted by a famous TV anchor with a mike: what did we think of the Starr Report? It was breaking news, and all the students spoke into the mike, on camera, with a poise that came from years of suburban assurance, and I said to them, when it was over, "How many other teachers get you on TV?"

And then there was the night when I was eight when Dad failed to come home. Just months before, he had bought a new, silver Firebird convertible. We'd put the top down, cruise around, and put the top up (that was a day's play). He always said he could never afford that car, but he bought it anyway. It stood out like an open zipper on the dull street of my third grade. And then, one night, he did not come home. We went to bed. Mom woke me up at six or seven in the morning to say that he'd been in a bad accident, but he was fine. What happened? He had gone to a meeting—an investment club? a teacher's union thing? a temple board group?—and when it was over, the car wouldn't start. He had called for a tow, was sitting on the hood smoking a cigarette, when something possessed him to get back inside. And then the crash. A drunken driver, we were told, plowed into the parked car, with Dad inside it, sending the whole thing skittering down the block, the emergency brake still on.

The car was totaled (the first time I'd heard that word). Nothing salvageable. The next day, he went out and bought the dullest, most anonymous car he could find, a deep green Chevrolet Impala. And that summer, we drove to Boston in it.

Fifteen years later, after the divorce, we reconvened for my brother's Princeton graduation. Mom and I sat there in a dorm room, waiting for Dad to pick us up and take us to the ceremony, and she opened up.

"That accident. Please. There was no meeting. It had been a tryst. You know what he is. I knew it when we married. I brought him home to meet my mother after we were in the Brooklyn College production of *Blithe Spirit* together. She said to me, 'Who is this man who is an actor?' And at the wedding, Aunt Gussie came up to me and said, 'You know, he's a *fagelah*.' Well, what did I care? I wanted to get out of that house, and he married me. My father was sick. God, how I still miss him. He sold chocolates and smoked cigars. He taught himself to sing by listening to John McCormack records. He loved to dance. Six weeks after I married, he was dead.

"To his credit, your father got me going after that. He forced me to finish college, forced me to get that master's degree, shoved me out of the house to go to work. We had a good time, acting in the plays at night and then going to the Garfield Restaurant for cheesecake. But then you were born, and then your brother, and everything changed. He was never home. And when he was, he brought his boys with him. The year you were born, he was teaching a ninth-grade class at Huddie Junior High, and all the kids chipped in and got you a blue blanket. I still have it. They were your first babysitters. Then they became his friends. It was fun at first, but after a while I knew what was going on and resented it. He'd bring home these men, now in their twenties, and I'd have to make them dinner while they sat around, and I would have to watch them worship him. *Him*. A ninth-grade teacher.

"Here's what I think: one night he was going off to meet someone, and someone else had heard about it and they set out to get him. Someone tried to kill him plowing into the parked car like that. Maybe it was one of those boys, or an angry dad, or somebody from school he made a pass at. It doesn't matter. I'm telling you, that's why we moved to Boston. How he got into Harvard is a mystery to me. And the only way he got that degree was because the dean of the school, who saw right through your father, was killed in a plane crash. So they had to give him the degree. You wonder why he couldn't get a job back in New York? Everybody knew.

"It was no better in Boston. Those families we spent those horrible Thanksgivings with—do you think those kids knew about *their* fathers? There was that Frenchman and his family, and every chance he got he'd hug Larry and say things like, 'I love you like a madman.' And then there was that Englishman who worked in the local school system. Do you remember that big old house in Cambridge? Dad loved that man because he had an accent and an eye patch. When he first introduced me to him, I thought he looked like Claude Rains. Your father probably thought so too. You and your brother and the other kids were upstairs watching TV, and the four adults were downstairs, cleaning up the dishes, and their hands touched.

"We could have had a life in Boston, too, but your father couldn't let it go. He did get one job offer out of grad school, at the school of education at Texas A&M. I remember he came back from the trip, and his advisor came to dinner: Dr. Hunt, a wonderful man, a Texan, Eisenhower's assistant secretary of education, a decent, decent man. He turned to Larry and he said, 'If you go to College Station there will be a cross burning on your lawn the first night. Think of your children.' And Larry thought he was talking about being Jewish.

"If you ask me, the only way he got that job in Pittsburgh was he slept his way into it.

"The man was a liar. And a terrible driver. I can't get into a car with him, the way he talks and tailgates and weaves around. Is he really going to pick us up? I'd rather walk. It's a miracle he hasn't died in a car."

He died in a hospital bed. He had gone in for heart-valve surgery, his voluble Argentinean surgeon assuring me that it was all routine. My father introduced me in Yiddish as *mein zindel,* the surgeon smiled and babbled something about *nachas, yichas,* and *sachel.* He shook my hand and six weeks later—after losing thirty pounds, after a regime of Coumadin, after two return visits to have his heart restarted—my father checked himself into the emergency room with back pain and just stopped living on the gurney.

I found the hospital and parked illegally on a side street, went in at the first door I saw, and found a desk. "My father passed away. I'm here to see the body." The nurse looked at me, unfazed, as if I were picking up my dry cleaning. She asked my name, got on the phone, and soon directed me to a room in another wing. An elevator, two hallways, a double door, and then a suite of rooms around a nurse's station. I mentioned his name. "Are you his brother?" No, I'm his son. Now she looked at me as if I'd lied, but she got up and walked me to the room, pulled back the curtain, and left me there.

He lay in the bed on his back, his mouth open, his skin the color of old parchment. It was as if they'd hooked a vacuum pump to his navel, drew the air out of him, and then left him on the mattress.

The doctor came in, a full ten years younger than me, shaken, his collar unbuttoned and his tie loose. "I'm very sorry. He came in last night with back pain, and we thought it might have been a kidney infection, so we put him on an IV drip of antibiotics and rehydrated him, and let him sleep." Now, reading from the chart: "The nurse checked in on him at noon today, and he was ready to go home. But when she came back fifteen minutes later he was cyanotic, in respiratory failure, asystolic. He was carted without response, and we declared him at 12:20. Do you want some time with him alone?"

I signed the forms and authorized an autopsy.

I walked out of the hospital and found my car. A sodden parking ticket stuck out from under the windshield wiper, and I tore it up. Now it was pouring rain, the San Francisco streets pitched up like waterslides. I inched out of my illegal spot, turned up the hill, and drove to his apartment building.

When Dad moved to San Francisco six years earlier, he wanted a great address — a number and a street that, when he mentioned it to someone in a store or on the phone, would cause them to gasp or smile and recognize him for the master that he'd hoped to be. The same as when he got his Harvard EdD, he put "Dr. Lawrence Lerer" on his checks and flew as "Dr. Lerer" — until one day (he'd regaled me with the story), someone had a heart attack on a plane, and he was called up to assist. It was certainly a good address: a 1930s, faux-Spanish apartment building on the corner of Pacific Avenue and Fillmore Street. With its wrought-iron gate, its Mexican tile floor, and its arched mosaic lobby, it looked, at street level, like a set for a Zorro movie. But the apartments were tiny and unrenovated. His still had the 1930s kitchen, with a big white porcelain sink and enameled stove; the living room had old sash windows; and the bathroom had the black-and-white tile of a chessboard. When I first saw the place, the day he moved in, I thought — well, that's it, he's finally found a place that looks like where he grew up. I changed my mind, the year before he died, when I was watching local news on TV. There was the building, and a reporter, and a story about a couple who kept pit bulls in their apartment, one of which had attacked another tenant, a woman in a same-sex relationship, and about how the whole building was full of gay men and women and run like a private club.

The day he moved in, I took him to lunch. He wore a four-hundred-dollar merino sweater, square tortoiseshell glasses, a gold bracelet, and a heavy ring. The maitre d' looked us up and down, like he was reading a Chinese newspaper, and then sat us in the back, as far away from anyone as possible. The waiter came over, and before he could open his mouth, Dad took his arm and said, as sincerely as he could, "Can you believe my son is taking me to lunch?" "If that's your story," he shot back.

I had no key, and I stood there in the rain ringing the manager's bell till she came out and I introduced myself and told her he was dead. She threw her arms around me, told me how much everyone in the building had loved him, gave me a spare key, and told me I could come and go as I wanted.

The elevator jerked me up, I got off, and walked into the apartment. A half-filled coffee cup sat on the dinette table. Bowls still flecked with cereal were stacked in the sink, the bed was unmade, a *Newsweek* was open on the couch, and the red light on the answering machine was flashing. I played the messages. "Larry baby, this is Miguel. Where were you last night? You know how much I miss . . ." I stopped it and erased the tape. I rifled through his desk, looking for anything to anchor me. His address book and calendar popped up, a thick, brown-leather Ghurka thing. I didn't open it; I smelled it. I picked it up and brought it to my nose and there was his smell, the smell he had always had, as long as I remembered, part tart cologne, part cigarette, part sweat. I split it like a bean. There was his handwriting, the same as always, with the large curved *L*'s, the open *a*'s, and the flourish at the end of each name. November 6: Tony, 5 pm. That was today. I flipped back: names and times, no details, no addresses. Weeks of one-named assignations.

I must have made thirty phone calls, sitting at his desk. I called the students from the 1950s, all of them neatly entered under their last names, all with updated numbers and addresses. "He was my best friend." "He was remarkable." "Just tell me where and when, and I'll be there." "I loved him." And then, the one piece of advice: "You know, Seth, at this moment, there is nothing you can do that will be wrong. Act on your instincts." And so I made a list.

Call his brother.
Call his boyfriends.
Get the password for his e-mail.
Call his lawyer and accountant.
Call his only living cousin.
Call Mom.
Call my brother.
Cancel class for next week.

There was no love in those calls. "I'm sorry for your loss." "It was bound to happen." "I'll get you the papers." "He was the stone in my shoe." The closest thing to missing him came from his cousin, who just blurted out, "That son of a bitch. How dare he die and leave me all alone?"—this from a woman he had not seen in twenty years.

I watched the rain spittle across the windows, thinking how he had been exiled from his own family, how he lived in his little island with his woodblock prints, his aunt's old silver, sepias of his grandparents, Bokharas, needlepoint pillows, and a large Erté sculpture stuck like a ship's prow right in the middle of the living room. I planted myself on the barque of his bed, surveying the horizon of the half dozen books on his shelf (two of which I'd written, two more of which I'd given him). The play we had talked about that morning repeated in my ears, each broken line reminding me of him:

> *My father's of a better nature, sir,*
> *Than he appears by speech.*

I got up and opened the closet. There were a hundred shirts, all pressed and still in their dry-cleaning bags. There were—I counted them—twenty-four pairs of shoes. There were a dozen cashmere scarves, thirty belts hanging on hooks. There was a shelf of hats: flat woolen caps, broad-brimmed fedoras, baseball caps, a Stetson. I pushed aside the rack of suits and there, behind them, on another rack, were fur coats, reaching to the floor. There were half a dozen leather jackets, leather vests, and leather pants. Three shopping bags were stacked against the back wall. I poured them out. A spiked dog collar rolled out first, then a whip handle, long steel chains, a set of cuffs. Wrapped in a towel was a disassembled rack. I reached in and pulled up a handful of matchbooks: the Stud, the End Up, Badlands, Moby Dick.

Look what a wardrobe here is for thee!

I found an inlaid wooden box, a crust of cocaine still inside it. In his drawer, I found a roll of twenties, four hundred dollars. I pulled everything out. Turning back to the desk, I sliced through the papers: threatening letters from a spurned lover, a restraining order against someone else.

Rough magic, robes, utensils, things of darkness.

Are you not my father?

The buzzer rang, and a tall, balding man with a thick Irish accent stood at the door. He introduced himself as one of the building's custodians, and he said right away that he had heard about my father's death, he was so sorry.

"Larry was a great tenant and such a wonderful friend, and I know this will seem strange right now, but he promised me his car."

His car?

"Yes, I'd like his car."

Now?

"Well, yes. I'm going away for the weekend, and I'd really like to have his car."

Look, I just got here and I can't give you his car. I can't even find his will. Let me settle the estate and then we can talk.

"Oh. Can I at least have the keys to borrow it for the weekend?"

All right, sure, bring it back on Monday, and if it isn't here I'll call the police and tell them you stole it.

It was a tiny Celica convertible, all black. Dad barely could get in and out of it, it was slung so low to the ground. The last time he drove to my house, I met him at the driveway, and he had to grab his thighs to lift his legs out of the pedal-well and plant them on the ground before he could haul himself out of the seat. Like Franklin Roosevelt getting out of bed, I thought. Once up, though, he could steady himself, though he still had his hand on my shoulder. That afternoon, he got me and my then-ten-year-old son to squeeze inside (me in the front, the boy, beltless in the luggage space behind the seats). He swung out of the driveway, turned, missed two stop signs, and shot up the highway ramp. He crossed two lanes, put it in fifth, and hugged the median like a slot car. We went as far as one of the exits that took us into wooded hills, curved around horse paddocks and Christmas tree farms, crested the skyline drive and caught a glimpse of bay and ocean out of each window, before turning back along the hairpins into suburbs nestling in for dinner. Streetlamps were on, but he kept his headlights retracted, darting like a bat between the slower-moving sedans. Then he killed the engine, coasting to a silent stop before our driveway, less than half an hour after we had left.

"Let's go again!" my son cried.

I gave the Irishman the keys and thought, I hope he never brings it back, and closed the door.

TWO

The Abduction
from the Seraglio

I went back to his closet, looking for anything to make him human. I found his pictures in his private's uniform, his discharge papers, and a carbon copy of a posting to Camp Carson, Colorado. Some of the pictures were studio shots from Brooklyn, taken on leave. There he is in the khakis, with his pompadour and his nose too big for the rest of him. Some were snapshots, all with his mother or Aunt Mary—none with his father or anyone else. The documents reported an injury, a medical discharge, and putting the dates together, I realized that he had served no more than sixteen months and was out before D-Day.

He never talked about the army. Even Mom was surprised. "When I first met him," she began one evening, after they had been divorced for a decade, "he had been out three years and never said a word. Even in the late forties, Brooklyn College was full of men still in their military haircuts and their good posture, ready to light your cigarette and tell you everything about the service. I went to college hearing about Anzio and El Alamein, and once I went to the movies with a man, a very nice, tall fellow with a good smile, and when the lights went down and the music started to blare he broke into a cold sweat, said he had to go outside for a smoke, and never came back."

"To this day I've no idea what he did in the army. The young men would brag in the cafeteria, and he would just sit there, silent, smiling, and when faces turned to him he'd say something like he was an interpreter, or in intelligence, or that things were so sensitive he really couldn't say. All I knew was that he was drafted on his eighteenth birthday, tested out of combat duty, and spent part of 1943 at Fort Dix and part of 1944 at a POW camp in Colorado, translating for German prisoners. Aunt Mary told me once he called her every day from Colorado, begging her to get him out. She said eventually he injured his back during some exercise, and they just had to discharge him. One day I went through his stuff, old cartons that his mother had told me to take, and there were notes in something I couldn't read. They looked like classroom language notes, and I held them out, like they were love letters to another woman, and said something like, and what are these, and he said that after Fort Dix a few of the boys were tested for their language skill and he passed so high on the exam that they sent him to Princeton for the summer to study Turkish with Professor Hitti, as part of some diplomatic plan. But it fell through just a few weeks into the course, and so they transferred him to German, where they trained him to be an interpreter for the POWs. So the Turkish notes just sat there in a box. He didn't even know he had them anymore. He said that after all that work he could remember only one sentence in Turkish: *Bu odada kaç pencere vardir?*, which means 'How many windows are in this room?' What a strange thing to remember.

"That's all I know, really. You ask him."

I did. Years later, when I was teaching at Princeton, I called him up and asked him to tell me about the summer there, about Professor Hitti and what he studied. Princeton in the forties. Must have been amazing. Einstein was there, right? Everybody else was out at Los Alamos, but Einstein was there. Did you ever see him? What about Hitti? I've got a colleague now who remembers him. But all he said was, "It was a long time ago."

The only other bit of information I could glean was when he blurted out one afternoon in Palo Alto, while I was barbecuing and our son, then two or three, was digging in the backyard, that watching him dig reminded him of his friend Moe, who went through basic training with him and then spent a hundred and forty-seven days in a trench on a Pacific island, and then met him in San Francisco after they were both discharged and rode back on the train all the way to New York with him.

I stood up with his army photos in my hand and looked up at his walls, plastered with pictures of himself. There was a set of photos from the Washington Opera's 1985 season, when they did Mozart's *Impresario* as a curtain-raiser for *The Abduction from the Seraglio*. Dad managed to get himself the two nonsinging roles: the first, the Impresario himself (*Der Shauspieldirektor*, a title he would spit out more like Yiddish than like German), and then the Pasha from the Seraglio (*Die Entführung aus dem Serail*, a title even he could not whip his tongue around). One of the photos, in garish color, had him draped in gold and red sateen, with a lopsided turban and his arms out, like he was welcoming applause for simply showing up.

Couldn't even carry a tune, I thought, famously tone-deaf, to the point where even the one song he could just barely sing—"Blue Moon," with its repeated notes and simple scale—wavered like an old record on the Victrola, running out of spring.

I looked out his window, and the rain blew against the glass like the sound of a Janissary's drum.

———

That fall (I imagined), it rained every day in Colorado, sweeping across five hundred miles of plains until it shattered against the barracks. He would wake up every morning, lather and pretend to shave, and then stand with the staff sergeant for roll and for inspection, and then they would troop the prisoners out in army-green buses to the wheat fields. Groups of boys, most no older than he was. Someone must have figured that months on the prairie would drive everybody nuts; they had to find something for all of them to do, prisoners and guards. And so they bused them out to the great farms in the flatlands, where they dug the wheat rows in the spring, then cultivated in the summer, and then in the fall scythed their way across, an army of fieldhands, marching in stubble.

He would sit with the prisoners in the buses, turning the sergeant's bark into the vowels they could understand. He'd sit, still, in the bus while they went out and cut the stalks, sometimes standing in the open door smoking a cigarette, sometimes running into the wheat field when a prisoner had to pee, to walk him to the pit latrine across the stubble, standing with him, his hand on a sidearm he never fired.

That night, after the canned ham and potatoes, he would stand in line at the base phone, waiting to call Mary, waiting to tell her how horrible it was, how he was so much younger than everyone else (or so it seemed) and how they taunted him, and how the sergeant called him in because someone had found one of Moe's letters, and the sergeant stood there with the letter, open in his hand, reading it like it was a map of an invasion, interrogating him about his loyalty, about this man's army, about Aunt Mary. He knew Aunt Mary knew people (I know people, you always said), and maybe she could write a letter or get an appointment with an important person. He missed Princeton, with its summer leaves brushing against the leaded windows of the lecture hall. He missed Professor Hitti, who lectured about how the Europeans got everything they knew from the Arabs, and how he ran the language classes like an orchestra conductor, leading them all in unison until, occasionally and without warning, he'd point at someone and get them to stand up and solo a sentence:

Bu odada kaç pencere vardir?

But Mary would just listen and remind him of his duty and remind him not to let anyone know, and yes, you have to eat the ham, and just don't do anything you'll regret, and we're all thinking of you, even your parents.

That night, like every night, he'd hang up and walk back, fighting against the wind and the rain (six feet tall and a hundred and forty-seven pounds), to the barracks, and he'd think, what can I do, what can I do now? And he'd figure that he'll do it next week, when they put all the enlisted men through the obstacle course, just to keep them in shape. By now, he can go through the course in his sleep (and does, waking up in a cold sweat out of a dream): the run through the tires, the scattering across the wet ground under the poles, the rope swing, the zigzagging through the dummy minefield, the climb up the wooden wall with the knotted rope, up, up thirty feet, then swing your left leg, then your right leg, over and then down, rappelling on the other side, and then more mud.

The next six days were glacial. Roll, the ride, the scything, seemed to take longer and longer. The sky pelted rain, and the prisoners would come back into the bus dripping wet, bits of stalk and awn stuck to their uniforms. He remembers a day, years ago, when Mary showed him her dresses and laid each one out on the bed, and he touched them, and she told him how the little patterns had been put on specially, in an extra-special way. *Appliqué.* He looks at the soldiers covered in rain-glued wheat bits and mouths, silently, the word. *Appliqué.* Nobody looks at him. By this point, they've learned not to look, though every now and then his eyes meet those of one of the prisoners, and they lock on, if only for a second, and then turn away, and his skills as a translator are needless.

His letters come, now already opened, fingered across Aunt Mary's fountain-pen script. Moe knows not to write anymore. Everyone long before stopped asking if he had a broad back home. Even the sergeant couldn't give a shit now, and it's just two days before drill.

He knew about it, first, from one of the prisoners, who would sing a little in the field and who, in the bus, was just about the only one who smiled. They shared a cigarette by the pit latrine. *Die Entführung aus dem Serail,* he called it. *O, ist es schön, wie lyrisch, wie komisch! Ich habe es geshen,* he began, and in a German finer than any of the other men's, he told him about the performance he had seen at the Vienna State Opera, in 1942, with the great Elisabeth Schwartzkopf.

The opera begins, he said, with Belmonte in search of his beloved Konstanze, who had been taken by pirates and sold into servitude to the evil Pasha. There is the manipulative servant of the Pasha, Osmin; the beautiful servant of Konstanze, Blonde; the clever servant of Belmonte, Pedrillo. There's so much, he went on, but the great moment is in act 2, when Konstanze laments to Blonde that the Pasha is in love with her:

Martern aller Arten
Mögen meiner warten.

He listened as the prisoner recited the lyrics, barely getting them through the scrim of the eighteenth-century poetry and the prisoner's refined accent. "All kinds of tortures may await me," he translated in his head.

Nur dann würd' ich zittern,
Wenn ich untreu könnte sein.

"I would tremble only if I were untrue to him."

It's all very melodramatic, he thinks, and he isn't even sure he's gotten all the lyrics, but the prisoner acts out the whole thing, with Belmonte searching and Konstanze weeping and Osmin plotting. The opera ends, he concludes, when Belmonte and Pedrillo bring ladders into the Pasha's garden, Osmin finds them, and then by a twist of plot, the Pasha—and here he can barely follow the long German sentences, with their built-up adjectives and final verbs—lets them go, while Osmin laments that he can't have them all killed.

Können Sie ein wenig singen? He asks, and the prisoner turns to him, stubs out his cigarette, and tries a few bars of the tenor aria:

Konstanze, Konstanze
Dich wieder zu sehen, dich.

He sings in a thin, sweet voice, the mist puffing from his mouth, the steam rising from the open pit latrine.

The opera, he goes on, catching his breath, was a great success, *ein grosser Erfolg,* when it opened, what with all things Turkish *der letzte Schrei* ("all the rage"; he knew the idiom) and the music full of Janissary drums. Mozart wrote too, did you not know, the famous "Rondo alla Turca" as the final movement to his sonata in A, another appeal to the taste for Turkish things. The Pasha kept his harem in a special room, called an oda, and Mozart's audience loved all the innuendos about sex and savagery.

And he says, I know, *Turkisch kan ich ein bisschen. Aber oda bedeudet nur Zimmer, nicht wahr?*

Ja, aber das oda des Paschas—das war ein bestimmtes Zimmer.

Oda, a special room, a room for women only, a room where the wives would lie on their special couches (*divans,* he remembered), waiting for the pasha to select one, waiting to be summoned for her duties. *Odalisque,* he remembers now, the woman lying on the couch.

And he remembers Professor Hitti, surveying his students, lecturing about the fineries of the Arab world, drumming into their heads the idea of agglutination in the Turkish language, pounding on the lectern, no, no, no, the particles agglutinate into grammatical units, and then his eyes, brown as sardonyx, glint, and he steps away from the lectern and points a finger right at him:

Lerer—Bu odada kaç pencere vardir?

That morning he gets up, even before the bugle, with the lyrics in his ears. His uniform is smarter than usual, the shirt and the green tie crisper, and the trousers—which he carefully laid out the night before under his mattress—pressed to a knife edge by his body. There's mess, and roll, and then the sergeant rounds up the enlisted men for drills, and then the obstacle course, just to keep them trim, the sergeant says, and everybody notices how eager he seems this morning. He grabs his rifle, holding it across his body like a weapon (Lerer, it's a weapon, not a pet), and he runs faster than anyone else, his feet dancing through the maze of tires, his calves going up and down like pistons, and he throws himself into the mud, loves the mud, keeps his weapon up and out of it, and then flips it around so it hangs from his back by the strap, and he grabs the knotted rope and climbs, fast, faster, with just his forearms hauling himself up out of the mud, and the rain beats on his face, and he gets to the top and throws his leg over the wall, and he grabs on to the knotted rope on the other side and straightens his legs against the wet wall, and he can feel the pride the sergeant finally has in him, and he knows he's ahead of all the other men.

And then he lets go.

One of the corporals told him once, over mess, how he had heard that when you parachuted out of a plane, it was like time stopped. You couldn't feel yourself falling, at first. You thought you were holding still and the plane was flying away from you. You just hang there, so you think, and so you have to count out loud, 'cause if you don't you'll just lose track of time and be splat on the ground before you know it. You have to count out loud, and when you hit ten, you pull the ripcord and the chute opens. You feel yourself yanked up by the chute. That's the first time you feel yourself moving. Funny, you know. You're falling, down, down, down, and the first thing you feel is being pulled up. And then, and only then, you can look down and see where you're supposed to land. You've gotta be real careful, gotta make sure you let your legs kind of crumple out under you, otherwise you'll just snap 'em like a twig. Then you roll over, stand up, pull up your chute, and hope that all this time no one's shooting at you.

That's how it's going to feel, he thinks, but without the chute. He'll just hang there, not looking down, and there'll be no chute and no one shooting at him, and he'll be free.

But he isn't. He lets go and he drops like a sack of potatoes, feels himself dropping, the air knocked out of him. Thirty feet. Lands on his keester, plop, right in the mud, a big splash. He sinks down about a foot. The whole thing happens in no time. The men are howling. Pointing. Bent over, hands flat out on their knees. Everyone. Except the sergeant. He knows. He walks over, a sad smile on his face, not bothering to quiet the men. You, and you, he points. Get this soldier to the infirmary.

He lies there in the bed, his back in a brace. They've given him some morphine for the pain. Nothing but pain really, just a sprained back. Lucky you fell on your keester, the medic says, between drags on a smoke. Jeez.

No one visits him. There's a letter from Mary, wishing him to get better, and a pack of cigarettes on the nightstand, and a basin on the floor. He listens for the scrape of a ladder against the outside wall. Nothing.

His eyes open, and he looks around. He tries to raise his head, but it just falls back against the pillow. He counts, aloud, in Turkish: *bir, iki, üç, dört, beş. Beş,* he says. *Beş.* There are five windows in this room.

Two weeks later, he gets off the bus in San Francisco, his discharge papers in his pocket.

THREE

Enter Tubal

I walked down the stairs and drove home in the rain. Twelve hours later I was in the parking lot of the Neptune Society. As far as I knew, Dad had left no instructions beyond the DNR, and so I called to have him cremated. Their offices were at the San Francisco Columbarium, a freakishly ornate structure overlooking the park. Built in the late nineteenth century, it was arrayed with niches for the ashes of the dead. Each of its ground-floor rooms was named for one of the mythic winds. There were stained-glass windows of angels and a fountain in the courtyard.

The Neptune Society devoted itself to the care and cremation of the dead. They would take care of everything, they told me on the phone: they'd oversee the body after autopsy, handle death certificates, and manage the cremation and the ashes.

A girl too pretty for the job sat at the front desk, took my name, and walked me over to a small room where I wound up working with a tall thin man with slicked back hair, long sideburns, and a face that looked like it had not seen daylight in a year. He rubbed his hands together, muttered something about returning to the earth, and then gave me a catalog with illustrations of the caskets and the urns that I could purchase. Ornate oak, walnut, and inlaid caskets ranged themselves on the pages. Some were adorned with gold leaf, others had silver fittings. Pictures of carved urns punctuated sentences such as: "Positive identification of the deceased is verified throughout each stage of the cremation process." I looked up, visibly unsettled by the thousand-dollar price tags.

"Here at the Columbarium," he began, "many of our clients value the attention that we give to detail. This a time of challenge for the loved ones, and we offer all the services that take the burden off their shoulders and enable them to say farewell as fully as they can. We can, if you like, arrange a scattering. Of course, if you wish scattering at sea, we'll need to do some paperwork. And if you move with the remains, you'll need to file a report with the state. You cannot bury them yourself; that's the law. We still have niches here available. As you may know, some of the city's finest citizens are interred here. Mayor Taylor's family insisted on his resting at the Columbarium. The Klumpke sisters had their ashes placed here in the 1940s—Dorothea Klumpke was one of the first female astronomers, and I often look up and think of how our Columbarium looks more like an observatory than a mausoleum. Harry Jansen is here. He used to be known as Dante the Magician; he coined the phrase 'Sim sala bim.' And, of course, Harvey Milk's ashes rest here. People come from all over the world just to look at his name."

I thought of Dad resting with Harvey Milk, with forgotten magicians and astronomers, his ashes shelved behind the marbled winds. I thought of spending thousands on his casket and his urn, burning up the inheritance just to let him know I could, wishing him back alive, to witness this macabre play and to see if, just once, he wouldn't hit on the attendant.

"Our clients like to know that they have done their best for the deceased, that they have not skimped, even at the end. Yes, it is true that the casket is incinerated. But how can you put a price on peace of mind?"

I ordered the cheapest thing in the catalog, a hundred-dollar plywood box, and for the ashes I asked for a plain wooden container with his name on it. He looked at me with all the dour dismissal of a character in a Charles Addams cartoon, but took my check and wrote down the particulars.

That afternoon, I let the estate agent into the apartment. There was a grad student at Stanford who had heard Dad died, and she was quick to let me know she had a cousin who handled estates. After all, she said, how much of his stuff was I going to keep? I opened the door and let the agent in before me. She stood still in the hallway, her eyes falling on the big Erté sculpture in the middle of the living room; on the walls of Japanese woodblock prints; on the pictures of his mother and his aunt; on the bogus Picasso, the big needlepoint pillows, and the Bokharas. "Your Dad was . . . ," she began, but then paused.

Yes, he was.

She got her pad, pencil, and calculator and began to inventory everything. She had an early version of a digital camera, and took pictures of the walls, the furniture, the floors, the closets. She pulled down the Picasso, only to let me know that these things were not really very rare, even if they were real. "At least," she laughed, "it's not a Dalí." We went through the drawers of watches, almost all of which she let me know were knockoffs. We went over the furniture, we lifted up the rugs, we counted up his hundred and twenty shirts, his shoes, his belts. I asked if it was worth a lot, how much, just ballpark, she thought.

"Look," she said, "most of this isn't worth very much. I'm sorry to have to tell you, but a lot of the artwork is either very common or dubious. What did he pay for these Alishinskys? I can't imagine getting more than a couple of hundred for them. The jewelry is nice, and some of it is real, but there's no market for men's jewelry in my business. The Japanese woodblock prints are cut out of old books and mounted. I doubt that I could get much for them.

I could sell the furniture, the kitchen stuff, and all the clothes to a consignment place tomorrow, no problem. Most of the silver seems very personal. Forget it. Keep the rugs. They're in good shape, but the colors are too striking for most people's tastes. And I don't know what you're going to do with that Erté."

She left, saying that she could let me know the estimate in a few days. She'd go online to confirm the prices and the chances of a sale, and get a sense of just how real his stuff was. But the kinds of people who would come to buy the stuff, she let me know, would respond more to notices in the newspaper and flyers on the doors. She'd like to have a day to keep the apartment open, just so people could walk through. She'd take twenty percent of the total sale. And, oh, yes, she was bonded.

That evening, I held court in the apartment. The long-term friend came by, a man now in his sixties whom I first met thirty years before, when he was blond and tan and thin and spoke in an Oklahoma accent like warm molasses. A new friend from the city stopped in, Turkish, in a crisp button-down shirt, his graying hair manicured into a short mane. They both knew each other, but moved warily around the apartments, like cats seeking out a turf.

"Larry was hopeless with machinery," the old friend began. "I knew him for thirty years, and he could never seem to turn anything on. When he moved in, he called me to set up his stereo. I put the whole thing together, programmed his favorite radio stations, put in a CD, turned it on, and said, 'Happy?' A month later I was back here and the same CD was in the changer. As for e-mail—he could barely use it. I'll give you his password, but I doubt you'll find anything. He never wrote to anybody and my guess is all you'll find is spam. The thing you'll want to do is call his lawyer and get the will cleared up. Then you'll want to go to the bank. I'll show you where he kept the safe deposit box key. Don't worry about the credit cards. Most of them were in my name, anyway, and besides, Larry loved walking around with cash. Most days, he'd have two or three hundred dollars on him. The one thing he was careful about, though, was checks. He had an old-style checkbook, with the stubs that stay in when you tear a check out, and he kept boxes of them. I'm sure you'll find them, though I don't know what you'll do with them.

"I know a lot of the names in his address book, but not everyone. Let's face it, he had a limited repertory: Jackson Fillmore for dinner, the Marina at sunset, movies at the Kabuki, Yerba Buena, morning coffee at Tully's down the street, the gym. After a while, everybody knew the script, and so he had to find new people to impress.

"The most important thing you need to understand about your father was that he was terrified of being alone. It wasn't so much that he needed company but that he needed an audience. Just being there to watch him order the veal chop was enough; and then to nod when he asked, 'Is yours good?' and then to force down a big dessert because he wanted you to eat. He loved to send presents. Only thing was, he would call you right away to make sure that you got it; never gave you a chance to write a thank-you note, or call him first. I always told him that he shouldn't drive that little car around the city, so he took the bus. We'd sit there, and he'd talk to me, but loud, and his eyes would dart around to see if everybody else was listening, and if he caught a glimpse of someone eavesdropping, he'd turn and talk to them. One day he got off in Japantown, and I swear he expected the other passengers to applaud.

"He was shattered when nothing theatrical turned up. You remember he had done all that theater in DC. Look at his walls, the pictures from the shows: there he is as Van Helsing in a *Dracula* adaptation; there he is as the Impresario and the Pasha in two Mozart operas; there he is as Tubal in *The Merchant of Venice*, the Folger Shakespeare Library performance. Nothing came up here;

well, you know there is no theater here, or none to speak of. And certainly nothing for him. He had a friend you've probably heard of, a studio executive, and Larry bugged him for a part—anything, a cameo, a walk-on. A couple of years ago he was jumping up and down that he was going to get something in an Adam Sandler movie—the old man that Sandler's character picks up and carries across the street to impress his son. He wouldn't stop: what should I wear, how should I walk? Like he was auditioning for *Hamlet*. Then he came over one night, more laughing than crying, to say that the producer called: 'Hey, Larry, sorry about the part; Adam wants a black guy.'

"Oh, and those hats. I never saw him wear any of them, either."

Would you like something personal of his?

"Like what."

But then the other friend piped up, that he had been with Larry when they bought the Picasso lithograph. He recalled, too, how Larry used to let him wear his watches, and how he had always admired a silver Cartier. I took the Picasso off the wall—six lines, evoking a face—and gave it to him. I rifled through a drawer and found thirty watches. Most of those are fakes, the friend said. I pulled the whole drawer out and presented it to him, like a doorway mother offering a bucket full of candy to a trick-or-treater.

Take the one you want.

And the old friend sat silently, embarrassed that he never wore any of Larry's watches.

I'll tell you what, I said to him. I'm going to go out for a while and run some errands in the neighborhood. You have a key. I'll be back in a couple of hours. Take anything you want and go. And get rid of all that equipment in the closet.

I walked down the hill to a musty used bookstore. No one was inside, and I opened up the door to hear its attached bell ring in the dark. A short man with a mop of hair came out, looked at me as if I had disturbed some alchemical experiment, and slipped into the back room. There were a few fine-binding books, some shelves of "first editions," and a shelf of popular psychology. A small case had a sign above it, "Literature," and there was an old Shakespeare from the 1930s, cracked, with gaudy lettering and fading photographs of great performances inside. I opened to *The Merchant of Venice*, and saw the tempest at its start. Antonio, the merchant of the title, enters, sad and weary. Salarino tells him that his mind is tossing on the ocean; his ships, his merchandise, remain in doubt. "Thou know'st that all my fortunes are at sea."

I sat down in a corner, looking for the Jew, the famous speeches, and for Tubal. I'd seen the play on TV years before, and when I was at Oxford I went to an outdoor performance at New College in which all the parts (in supposed Shakespearean authenticity) were played by men. But I had no memory of Tubal. It took time, wading through seas of prose where Portia and Nerissa speak, long verse passages of plot exposition, and the confusions of all the stories Shakespeare wove together in the play. There was the story of the caskets, which I had completely forgotten: Portia's father "was ever virtuous,"

Therefore the lottery that he hath devised in these three chests of gold, silver, and lead, whereof who chooses his meaning chooses you, will no doubt never be chosen by any rightly but one who you shall rightly love.

Shakespeare's prose was a nightmare to me, and I flipped over the pages, looking for familiar lines. Shylock, in this edition, was just called "The Jew," and I scanned down the page—Jew, Bassanio, Jew, Bassanio, Jew, Bassanio, on and on, until Antonio enters. "I am debating of my present store." He doesn't have the money. Ah, he needs Tubal to front him three thousand ducats. Now I understood what he was doing in the play. Now I read on, remembering the scenes on TV and at New College. I found the passage where the Jew demands his pound of flesh. I found the scene where the Moroccan picks the golden casket. I laughed out loud at the clowns, held my breath over Jessica. I was just into act 3 when I saw him: Enter Tubal.

Here comes another of the tribe.

Shylock then asks about Portia, and Tubal answers:

I often came where I did hear of her, but cannot find her.

I read the words aloud: about the flattest, most unpoetic line that I had ever seen in Shakespeare. And then, Shylock:

Why, there, there, there, there! A diamond gone cost me two thousand ducats in Frankfurt! The curse never fell upon our nation till now; I never felt it till now. Two thousand ducats in that, and other precious, precious jewels.

Amazing. There he is, in prose, and he's more powerful than anyone in verse. I read the lines over and over. I heard the climax in the repetitions—all the drama in those four *theres*, a heartache in a price tag, and a lifetime's pause between *precious* and *precious*. Tubal speaks, now only to be interrupted:

Tubal: Yes, other men have ill luck too. Antonio, as I heard in Genoa—
Jew: What, what, what? Ill luck, ill luck?

Tubal is full of information, but the Jew's words, in their simple, insistent repetitions, say far more. Again and again in this brief scene, Tubal tries to tell the Jew, as simply and prosaically as possible, that Antonio's fleet is lost, that Portia has spent Shylock's money in Genoa, and that she has sold off his turquoise ring:

I spoke with some of the sailors that escaped the wreck. . . .
One of them showed me a ring that he had of your daughter for a
  monkey. . . .
But Antonio is certainly undone. . . .

Empty lines, undramatic. It's Shylock who has it here, Shylock who iterates over and over, giving us what Shakespeare clearly must have seen as Jewish rhetoric: repetitive, insistent, every word a finger thrust in the air. "Good news, good news! Ha, ha, heard in Genoa!" And then, after this brief exchange, Shylock is done with him. "Go, Tubal," he says, three times at the scene's close, as if he can't wait to get him off the stage.

I closed the book and thought of all the things Dad could have said. I remembered the pictures on his wall, the roles he played at camp, with Mom in the suburban theaters of their pastimes. I remembered how he called me the last time he'd seen his own parents together, just before his father died, and he said, "It was like in Lear, two birds in a cage," pronouncing "Lear" as if it had three syllables. Did he audition for Antonio, all metered melancholy? Did he ask for Bassanio, all bonhomie? Or Shylock—would he have shown up at the call all nose, all accent?

I am a Jew. Hath not a Jew eyes? Hath not a Jew hands, organs, dimensions, senses, affections, passions; fed with the same food, hurt with the same weapons, subject to the same diseases, heal'd by the same means, warm'd and cool'd by the same winter and summer, as a Christian is? If you prick us, do we not bleed? If you tickle us, do we not laugh? If you poison us, do we not die? And if you wrong us, do we not revenge? If we are like you in the rest, we will resemble you in that.

I said those lines for him like a Kaddish, thinking of the collar and the chains, the leather and the spikes, the costumes of his company, begging that he be understood, begging that even for his faults he be forgiven. *If we are like you in the rest . . .* But he was not. He walked on, right after these lines, said his prose portion in the wake of Shylock's prowess, gave the news, and then was shooed offstage:

Go, Tubal, meet me in our synagogue.

I turned the page, and the edition showed a reproduction of a painting of the two of them, the old Jew with his beard and hooked nose, and his friend, with side-locks and his hands clasped in a moment of remorse. It was an eighteenth-century painting, but the poses looked like something out of silent film—arch, overacted. The Folger picture on his wall had the cast in modern dress: a black Antonio in a gray suit, a pudgy Shylock in a rep tie, looking for all the world more like a suburban Reform rabbi than a Shakespearean merchant. Where were the enchantments of a costume? Ten years after he'd dressed up as the Pasha, here he was, all prose in a suit he'd purchased for the part.

I remembered a day, several years before, when I took him to meet my Stanford colleague, a distinguished Shakespeare scholar, Jewish, from New York, close to Dad's age. He'd grown up on Park Avenue and had been openly gay, I gathered, since college. Since arriving at Stanford in the mid-eighties, he had lived in an exquisite home near the campus. Dad was in San Francisco by then, and he drove down in the black Celica to join me for tea at my colleague's house. We'll go in my car, I said, and we sidled through winding streets, mapped out for affluent physicians and business school professors, quietly pulling up to the house. The boyfriend let us in, a slight Japanese man, about ten years younger than I was, and he led us through the living room, past Rookwood pottery and Biedermeier furniture, past first editions of the modern poets, and through a glass door on to a cedar deck. There was a table, four chairs, and a teapot in a cozy. There were four china cups and saucers, and a plate on which four slices of date-nut bread had been fanned. My colleague was already sitting there, waiting for our courtesy, and I introduced Dad and talked about how he had been doing some acting, and wasn't it a pleasure, now that he had moved to San Francisco, that he could spend time with me and his grandson. My colleague put out his hand, a little surprised when Dad actually took it and shook it, and we sat down and had the tea, and each of us got a single slice of date-nut bread. It is a lovely garden, isn't it Dad, and you know my colleague has been such a good friend since I first arrived. But we got nowhere, and the boyfriend was visibly jealous of my attentiveness to his patron.

Finally, just to try and get things going, I began.

You know, it's always fascinated me how many of Shakespeare's great characters have only daughters and no sons. Prospero, Shylock, Lear. It's as if they couldn't bear the burden of male children, as if they must be the teachers or the keepers of their daughters, as if male identity figures itself against a woman who rebels. Being a parent in Shakespeare—I wonder if it had anything to do with his own sense of fatherhood, or his relationship to his own father. What do you think? Do you think his father really was a Catholic? Do you think his name was really Shakeshaft and he changed it? The father-daughter relationships are really the most powerful. I mean, after all, who really has a son in Shakespeare?

"Only clowns and kings," my colleague said, not looking at me, almost as if he were speaking to the tea.

Oh, right, of course. I got back on the horse. Remember *Henry IV, Part 1*, the scene where Prince Hal plays with Falstaff. "Do thou stand for my father." Or the bit at the end, where Hal and Henry meet at battle, and they finish each other's other lines.

I loved that bit. Yes, I guess there really are some good sons in Shakespeare. Prince Hal.

"Or Lancelot Gobbo," said the boyfriend, like he was letting air out of a tire.

The wind blew through the fruitless mulberry tree in the garden. A hummingbird passed by, held itself almost soundlessly at eye level, and finding nothing sweet or red nearby, flew off.

All this came back to me in the bookstore, and I flipped through to find the scene with Gobbo and his father from *The Merchant*:

Do I look like a cudgel, or a hovel post, a staff, or a prop? Do you know me, Father?

I scanned a few lines down:

Do you not know me, Father?

And then I remembered how the afternoon had ended: how I brought the conversation back to Dad as Tubal, how I told my colleague that he'd played in *The Merchant* at the Folger. And I was back, for a minute, in that garden.

I missed the show, but I've seen the pictures, really a terrific production.

"Really?" my colleague perked up.

And now my father: "Yes, it was a lovely production, all modern dress, remarkable cast."

"Yes, I'm sure. And how did you play Tubal?"

"Well."

———————

And at the close of *Henry IV, Part 1*, when Prince Hal and the King meet on the field of battle, he turns to his father:

And God forgive them that so much have sway'd
Your Majesty's good thoughts away from me!
I will redeem all this . . . ,
And in the closing of some glorious day
Be bold to tell you that I am your son.

FOUR

Blithe Spirits

I must have fallen asleep in the bookstore, and the owner poked me, wondering if I was buying anything that day. "We're not a library." You're not much of a bookstore either, I retorted, and then immediately realized my mistake. I'm sorry, my father passed away this week, and I've been thinking a lot about him. I described him to the owner and he knew him immediately.

"Oh, yeah. Old guy. Beard, leather jacket. Came in all the time. Never bought anything. I'm surprised he had a son."

He had two. And a wife.

His silence asked the question.

It's a long story.

"Business is slow."

My parents met as actors, in the Brooklyn College production of *Blithe Spirit* in 1948. Dad was in his early twenties, out of college, already with an MA and a teaching job. What he was doing back at Brooklyn College starring in stage plays with undergraduates was a mystery to me. But there he was, Charles Condomime to Mom's Ruth, the second wife. We have a picture of the cast, each member signing off under his or her costumed head—an assembly of Jewish immigrant children, convinced that the surest way to successful assimilation was to ape the artifice of 1930s British swells. Decades later, hardly a week went by when, sometime between the salad and the ice cream, Dad would yell out, "Damn you, Ruth," and Mom would get that look on her face as if to say, "Tell that silly old bitch to mind her own business." It was their play, and "Always" was their song. Without the slightest provocation, Dad would burst into its opening refrain, and he and Mom would do a turn around the kitchen and recall how Morty Gunty or Irwin Mazursky garbled their lines, couldn't act, and now, see how famous they became (Irwin having changed his name to Paul). And as the strains of "Always" filtered down the hall, the Brooklyn College Barrymores came back to life.

We had a theatrical life, and I was put onstage almost as soon as I could talk. Every summer, Mom and Dad would work the camps in upstate New York, Dad directing the plays, Mom doing the sets. When I was five, they put me in the camp itself—the kids' bunk at camp Kee-Wah—while they did the shows. Privileged arena for the Brooklyn aristocracy (that summer, the heir to the Waldbaum's grocery chain was a bed-wetting bunkmate, and the camp boasted such alumni as Lauren Bacall and Paddy Chayefsky), Kee-Wah offered up that blend of Jewish cultural instruction and athletic sadism so characteristic of the fifties summer experience. The camp was run by Isidore ("Izzy") Monees, a man who looked exactly like Mr. Magoo and whose name I always misunderstood as "easy money." He'd bark his orders to his minions and make unannounced spot-checks on bunks just to terrify us.

That summer when I was five, I had a counselor who was a medical student. He insisted on playing doctor with us—a whole bunkload of the barely toilet-trained. He'd bring out his stethoscope and reflex hammer at all hours, giving us exams (I think I had suppressed the horror of it all until, when my own son was five, I told him I had to go off and give my students an exam, and he said, "Will you use a stethoscope?"). There was also my Israeli accordion instructor. He would show up in sandals (the first man

I ever saw wearing sandals), play "The Flight of the Bumblebee," and then hand over the accordion. "Now, you play." At one point he said something in Hebrew about my performance, and I quit the accordion then and there.

But I could not get out of playing so easily. The year before, I wasn't even in the camp and Dad put me onstage. All I remember is that I was supposed to be a horse, and as I was running around the stage in a circle, the counselor playing the piano yelled out, "Seth Lerer." It was the only name I heard. Had she called everyone's name, or just mine? And the summer I was five I was a dog, the emcee of a talent show where everyone was dressed as animals. And I remember, too, another show when I was costumed as a doctor (I borrowed the counselor's stethoscope), with "Ben Crazy, MD," written on my smock. And even earlier—I must have been just three—there is a memory of Dad insisting that I put on a large diaper and get on a platter, trussed up like a roast pig with a tomato in my mouth, while the drama staff danced out intoning, "Larry Lerer, Larry Lerer, Larry Lerer," to the tune of the Hallelujah chorus.

His name, my name, they blend together. For years, I heard his name yelled out. Hardly a week went by in Brooklyn when I didn't hear a voice calling out, "Mister Lerer, Mister Lerer! Remember, *Kiss Me Kate*, 1954? Another opening, another show . . . ," and some poor pimpled adolescent would be going through the motions of a show my Dad had put on years before. It was as if he had taught, or directed, everybody. There were fat little boys and svelte women, on street corners, at newsstands, in Ohrbach's, everywhere. "Mister Lerer!" Once, years later, when I was a college student, we all went to Martha's Vineyard for the summer. Driving around, we found a bit of shore that turned out to be a nude beach. Of course, Dad had to drag us there; what an adventure. And my brother and I, now too embarrassed to say anything, and my mother, with that "It's child support!" look on her face, sitting there while Dad strutted around naked, deep in the narcotic of his exhibitionism. And then, from out of the surf, "Mister Lerer, Mister Lerer! Remember, *Kiss Me Kate*, 1954? Another opening, another show . . . ," and now a middle-aged fat man in a red beard, dancing along the sand, his genitals flying this way and that, a pendulum to mark the time.

Play after play, my parents marked their time. After we left New York in the mid-1960s, we moved to Boston, then to Pittsburgh. Suburban amateur groups, conditioned to the well-meaning posturing of Junior League matrons, would gape in awe at Mom and Dad's flamboyance. Whenever we moved into a new town, they would seek out the theatricals, much as someone else's parents might seek out the church or the good schools. The parts were all impostures. When we lived in Needham, Massachusetts, Mom and Dad starred in a local production of *The Rivals*. He was Captain Absolute, the dashing scion of the minor aristocracy, feigning to be young Ensign Beverley to woo Lydia Languish (Mom). Captain Absolute. The name became a clarion at home. For in the mid-1960s, TV was full of superheroes: Mr. Terrific, a mild-mannered clerk who takes a special potion; and Captain Nice, a momma's boy whose potent pill made him the Superman of the suburbs. Such shows should really be appreciated as the origin of camp, playful tales of effeminates who find themselves transformed for public maleness. Did Dad take a pill each morning? What were the potions of his public self? In those *Rivals* days, he would return from work and, entering the kitchen stage right, would announce, "It's Captain Absolute." And Mom, languishing in her days alone, would hide her secret novels and the LPs and make a dinner that he would never finish before charging out, quoting a line crushingly out of context:

No, no, I must prepare her gradually for the discovery . . .

He never did.

Another town, another show. Once, they played in *The Odd Couple*. Dad was Felix, the neat freak, and Mom was Gwendo-lyn — or Cecily, I always got them confused. Neil Simon's Pigeon sisters, I discovered later, had the same names as the ingénues in Oscar Wilde's *The Importance of Being Earnest*, a play my parents never did, but one they raved over in a performance at Stratford, Ontario, where the great William Hutt played Lady Bracknell in repertory one year with *King Lear*.

I'd often wondered if Dad would age into Lear or Lady Brack-nell, but there was no question about Mom. She remained born to play her part, Renée, named after Renée Adorée, a silent film star of the 1920s whom her father must have coveted. She stares out of the photo at her grandparents' fiftieth wedding anniversary, three years old with the look of a born performer: pouty, blank, covered in that ennui that years later would become the core of her Ruth. And there she is, in the portrait for her wedding, look-ing in a mirror and adjusting her veil. The camera catches her reflection, not her full face, and for all the world she looks less like a bride-to-be than an actress preparing for a part, surrounded by the mirror lights, the makeup, the costumes.

Mom rediscovered her theatrical gifts after she and Dad di-vorced. She'd moved back to New York, to Jackson Heights in Queens, but found it changed so much since her childhood that streets were barely recognizable. Old Jewish women jostled on the street with recent émigrés from Argentina. Colombian drug dukes (the lords were elsewhere) shared office space as bogus travel agents with south Indian accountants. Korean dry cleaners paid rent to Greek landlords.

One day, on a street full of saris, it occurred to Mom to join the Yiddish theater. What was left of the old legacy of Second Avenue was now ensconced in an Episcopalian church basement deep in midtown. The *Folksbiene*—the people's stage—had been revived, and Mom auditioned for a role in *Shop*, a bit of twenties agitprop that was selected as the troupe's seasonal opener.

When Mom got the part, and when the show was set, we agreed to see her. I drove in from Princeton with my wife, who found all this as much an anthropological venture as a family obligation, as if Margaret Mead had actually married one of those Samoans and was every now and then compelled to show up at some ritual of mutual humiliation. When we arrived, we found ourselves the only people in the audience under seventy, and we took our seats—under our own power—waiting for the play to begin. There was Mom, the young shop worker, speaking a stage Yiddish far removed from 1930s Brooklyn. The stage was filled with sewing machines nearly as old as the actors themselves, though I suspect the cast had more metal parts, not to mention plastic and batteries, than did the manual machines.

During the intermission, as my wife and I wandered around what had been conjured into a theater lobby, someone came up to us and asked, in Yiddish, what we were doing there. I noted that my mother was in the play.

Which one was she, he asked, and I said something to the effect of, Oh, the one on the right in the big chorus scene.

"Oh," he replied in English. "The ingénue."

She always was, whether performing or painting. Her art was as much a part of her as acting, and I grew up with her portraits and her still lifes. She painted brilliant circles on my bedroom walls, and one day after kindergarten she taught me to paint. Colors ran goopily from my brush, until she taught me how to hold it, how to get the watercolor on just right, and how, if you put a little bit of paint on one edge of the brush and turned it in a circle on the paper, you would get a little circle, shaded on one side and light on the other. I dipped the brush into the purple paint just as she showed me, and we painted grapes. They clustered on the shiny paper as they clustered in the backyard of our Brooklyn neighbors—an Italian family who actually had a grape vine and a fig tree (which they ritually bound in canvas every fall).

Mom learned to paint her canvas fruits at the Brooklyn Museum Art School under William Kienbusch, an abstract expressionist and scion of a wealthy Princetonian family. He was always "Mr. Kienbusch" in my mother's stories: elegant, well traveled, impeccably turned out. I Googled him and found his photograph from 1956: T-shirt, paintbrush, dark eyes, and a lower lip to die for. He seems to have spent a good deal of his time, when not teaching (according to the Smithsonian Archives of American Art website), traveling through Europe. Three volumes of his journals lie in the Smithsonian. They are in the form of letters to his mother, telling her of Spain and Greece, the Prado and the Parthenon. "He gives his impressions of Athens in long passages," notes the website, "and describes eating lunch with the Greek King and Queen and other guests at the exclusive Propeller Club."

Mom's only travels in those days were to the Brooklyn and Metropolitan museums, and the only royalty she dined with was the carpet king of Flatbush, who commissioned her to paint a circus mural in his house using his own face for the ringmaster. One day, she put my father in the circus. In a portrait she painted in the early 1950s, he is making up as a clown before an act. He's looking in the mirror, applying eyeliner, his face already whitened. The face is stretched out, as if to take the makeup more evenly, but I think that it's more a look of surprise than of preparation. The eyebrows raised, the mouth wide open. It's a look of fear, of fascination. How different from the serene Mr. Kienbusch, staring out from my computer screen, meeting my gaze, uncostumed, the paint confined to his canvas. What did my mother see in him? What did she see when she looked in the mirror of her wedding picture? What did my father see as he made up before a show?

As a child, I saw mirrors everywhere: windows at night, the

backs of spoons that made each dinner a fun-house, my reflection in Mom's eyes.

The TV sat in the den like a black mirror of my soul, until my father came home. Then we would spend the early evening watching game shows. *"Zu sugen, dem emes!"* he would shout in Yiddish, complete with a flourish of a hand, as if it were a magic spell. *To Tell the Truth*. That was his favorite, but they all were there: *I've Got a Secret, What's My Line?* The game shows of the fifties and sixties were all about finding out, all about exposing impostures of the everyday. Find the real violinist, the man who married a princess, the woman who can recite the Bible by heart.

But the truth was, these were game shows about us. The TV of the 1950s broadcast secrets. The Army-McCarthy hearings filled the screen in the year before I was born, and I grew up overhearing all my parents' arguments about the guilt or innocence of others. Are you now or have you ever been . . . ? Before McCarthy, there was Rapp-Coudert, a state legislative committee that held hearings on the "subversive attitudes" of New York public school and college teachers (this was in the early 1940s, but it was as fresh as Friday in my house). Inquests of this kind went on for a decade. My mother's favorite professor at Brooklyn College, Harry Slochower, had spent her whole undergraduate life under investigation for his "sympathies," and he was eventually dismissed in 1952.

We sat there in the den, watching domesticated versions of the trials my parents feared. The game shows deflected social terror. They channeled the anger and the fascination of a nation reared on loyalty oaths and security investigations, HUAC and "Red Channels." The urge to expose was still there, only now, under the benign and bow-tied aegis of Bud Collyer or Garry Moore, the stakes were simple.

I've got a secret. And the biggest secret was the sex behind it all. Just think about those black-and-white interrogators. Instead of Kefauver or Murrow, there was Robert Q. Lewis, Bennett Cerf, Peggy Cass, Dorothy Kilgallen—as sexually ambiguous a panel as you would find. Woody Allen lays all this out in one of his movie skits, where a rabbi comes on a game show and reveals his secret wish: to be tied up and beaten by a shiksa while his wife sits at his feet and eats pork. I've got a secret. What's my line? To tell the truth, it was always about desire: how could we transgress, and would they ever find out?

And then there was *Beat the Clock*.

We lived in the theater of interrogation, and my parents shaped their sympathies to fit their fears. There's an old joke my mother's cousin used to tell about the 1970s, when vans of young Ortho-dox men trolled the streets looking for lapsed Jews to enfold. "Are you Jewish?" they would ask strangers on the street. Those who weren't said, "No." Those who were said, "Who wants to know?"

We all wanted to know, and for my family Judaism was as much a play as anything else. There were the costumes of the faithful, the rites and rituals, the shows of Sabbath and Seder. For Reform Jews of my mother's generation, the great fear was not the gentile but the deeply observant. Her bitterness reserved itself for the believers of her own kind, and the New York of my childhood filled itself with bearded men and covered women I was taught to loathe. On day, Mom's mother went into the hospital. It was around the corner from the old Lubovicher seminary in Brook-lyn. Mom and Dad left me with my younger brother in the car. Now, I could not imagine leaving a pet in an unattended vehicle, let alone two boys, eight and four. But if I did, what would I say to them? Don't touch the dashboard, leave the wheel alone, keep the doors locked. No. From my mother it was, Don't look the Lubovich in the eye. We had these superstitions about them—that they wouldn't let you take their picture, that they wouldn't count off in gym class, that if they met your gaze you would turn into a goat. But I think what my parents really feared was that if they looked you in the eye they'd turn you back into a Jew. Assimilation, passing, whatever you called it, could be wiped away before what Mom feared was their terrifying gaze. They were the real spirits of my nightmares, and my earliest memory is of a dream in which my bed is surrounded by dancing flames, each with a leering, bearded face.

Maybe what terrified Mom most was that her children would be stolen. Abducted into orthodoxy, we would have denied her the salvation of her social soul. My son the doctor, my son the lawyer, my son who passes. I had a friend in high school who became a Chasid, much to the derision of my family. These were my father's fears as well. We'd have to do the passing for him, as, later in his life, we would show up at public events just to prove that he had children.

For us, it was always a costumed life, and from the wardrobe of my Judaism I'd put on one more. My brother was Bar Mitzvahed in suburban Pittsburgh in June 1972. By then, my parents were living so far beyond their means—a seven-bedroom stone house, a gardener, and a Mercedes—that one great fling would hardly dent their debts. Dad had a way of hearing about "the best" of everything. Friends, lovers, coworkers—somebody always told him about the best restaurant, or the best movie, or the best lawn service. Invariably, they turned out to be fly-by-night, or someone's brother, or a front for illegal operations (once, we turned up at a Polish restaurant in Pittsburgh where, it was immediately apparent, no one had eaten in years, there were no menus, and we had to be out by eight o'clock). As my brother's Bar Mitzvah rolled around, Dad came home with news of the best caterer in Pittsburgh. Sight unseen, food untasted, he retained them. We would have the ceremony at the temple in the morning, then come home and they would be set up, the party in the garden, everything in order. And so, when we turned the corner at one-thirty, we saw the big "Wilson's Catering" truck, and, emerging from it, a family of African Americans, in livery, toting great platters of ribs, ribeyes, roasts, and greens. A white-toqued server carved, and women in the kinds of maids' uniforms you see now only in pornography took drink orders. It was high theater all right, and for years all Pittsburgh talked about the Lerers' soul food Bar Mitzvah with the same blend of awe and horror as the court of Louis XIV must have talked about the king inviting Molière to sit in his presence.

All of which brings me back to Mom the ingénue, singing about a sweatshop on a borrowed stage. *Shop* was a play about the worker's plight, about illicit love among the sewing machines. But it was also a play about the theater itself: about the magic of material, about how immigrants cut the patterns of their lives out of the bolts, about how dress and drama always go together. Little wonder that its playwright, the pseudonymous H. Leivick, was also the author of *The Golem*—perhaps the most famous play in all the Yiddish repertory, a story of a monster conjured out of clay, a haunted creature, a miscreant. We all have ghosts and golems in our lives (could you imagine *Blithe Spirit* in Yiddish—*A Freyliche Geyst?*), and all that we can do is dress up in disguise or paint away the winter.

Years after Mom had given up the people's stage, she took to her apartment's walls in Queens and painted birds and branches. The wooden wardrobe, too, took on her colors, as a twig arched over the armoire and met its mate against the wall. My wife thought it looked so natural, but I knew that this was a stage set. Mom had painted herself in, transformed her flat apartment into a one-bedroom theater. "For God's sake," says the ghostly Elvira in the final act, "not another séance." But the door is open and the table set.

FIVE

Vaseline University

I finished my performance, and the bookstore owner turned to look out the window. Night had fallen. He had made no sales that day. He got up without speaking, opened the door and held it for me, his unkempt hair soon covered with the evening's misty spittle.

"Keep the book."

I hadn't eaten all day, and I walked up Fillmore Street toward his apartment, stomach growling. I passed the Tully's and the bank. I looked into the window of the Jackson Fillmore Restaurant and saw his empty seat. I walked in, told the waiter, my Dad used to eat here all the time, loved to sit in the window right there. Mind if I take the table? I'll be out in an hour.

I sat down facing his old seat, ordered the veal chop, and turned to his absence.

The spring of my senior year in high school, you disappeared for weeks. There were the business trips to New York and San Francisco, and whenever you would leave, I'd have to drive you to the airport just to keep the car. We'd get up at five so you could get the first plane out, as if you couldn't wait to leave, and I'd be back home by 6:30, barely knowing what to do until first period. One morning, I was so sleepy, you drove us both out (I would take the car back), and as you pulled up to the terminal, you stuck your hand out to adjust the side-view mirror and it fell out of its frame and shattered on the ground. The noise jarred me, and you shot me a glance, just to make sure I was awake, and threw yourself out of the car, not even closing the door, and then, turning in the terminal doorway, shouted out, "What do I care about a mirror? I make fifty-five thousand dollars a year," and spun on your loafer through the automatic door, as if "To Be Continued" were flashed across the screen.

You weren't there, that spring, when the thin envelopes arrived. Harvard, Yale, Princeton, Amherst—all of them wait-lists or rejections. My only package came from Wesleyan, to which I had applied late and listlessly, because you had a friend whose son had gone there in the 1960s and described it as a "fine school." No one in Pittsburgh in the early 1970s had heard of Wesleyan. There was Ohio Wesleyan, but that was not it. There was Wellesley, and every now and then someone would taunt me in my final weeks of high school: Wesleyan—isn't that a girls' school? And then there was your father, whom we visited that summer on the way to check out the campus. We stopped for an afternoon at the apartment in Brooklyn, the apartment in which your parents had lived since the 1940s, and Grandma Tillie boiled a steak with noodles and we sat around the tired kitchen while Grandpa Norman found his teeth, and then, when he asked where I was "attending college," he repeated the school's name over and over in his accent. "Vaseline? You're going to Vaseline?"

In the fall of 1973 I entered Vaseline University, armed with a box of opera LPs and a stereo, an electric typewriter purchased just for the occasion, and a handful of books. We all had private rooms in the dorm, and I dumped my stuff and found an open door. Unpacking there was a tall, brown-haired boy from Manhasset, who, as I entered, was hanging something up that looked to me like a bathrobe.

Cool robe.

"It's not a robe, it's my *gi*. For karate. You got any dope?"

Thirty-six hours later, we had heard that, dressed in his *gi*, this guy had jumped through a classroom window, screaming something that sounded like Japanese, and his room had been cleared out and vacuumed clean. I ran into the RA that afternoon, and jerked my thumb over to the guy's room.

"One down," was all he said.

After two days, another guy moved in—Phil, twenty-six, returning after, as he put it, "some time on my own," with an Irish wolfhound named Lucille that lived in the room and, rumor had it, had borne his child.

I'd signed up for a great books sequence, a yearlong course whose syllabus integrated history, philosophy, and literature, from Greek antiquity to high modernism, all to be taught by a team of faculty. The philosophy professor had hair down his back, wore a white turtleneck with a large medallion on a chain, and insisted that we take our shoes off and sit in a circle on the floor because "that's how the Greeks did it." The literature professor had just arrived, having received his PhD at twenty-four, and he liked to have us over to his apartment to listen to the Pachelbel *Canon* and talk about the books. We'd sit on his Goodwill furniture and drink white wine, and one time, when I wanted to impress him with my understanding of Greek theater, I got up and looked around and found him in the kitchen talking to one of the girls about his father's having been a Hungarian ambassador, and as she bent down I quietly turned and left and could never listen to Pachelbel again.

And as the snow fell in Connecticut, I would repeat the chorus of Aristophanes's *Frogs*, *brik-kik-kik-kax, koax, koax,* louder and louder just to see if I could get the image of that kitchen out of my mind. One morning I stepped out of the communal bathroom in the dorm to see a young man standing there, stark naked in the hallway, his blond hair falling over his eyes, his right hand brushing it up in a movement so natural and fluid that I thought, does he actually know he's naked. He caught my eye and stuck his hand out and said, half with a shrug and half with a toss of his head like Peter O'Toole in *Lawrence of Arabia*, "I'm Billy. I came here to act."

I didn't even know there was a theater department.

"There isn't."

In his room, wearing a silk robe and holding a burning cigarette (which he never brought to his lips), he laid out his plan to stage *The Importance of Being Earnest*. Billy would be Algernon, and he'd pull the cast together. He had the costumes already, of course, and the biggest challenge would be getting people *here* to memorize their lines, but he had worked with worse. I'd done some acting, I began, but he brushed me off with a bit of cigarette ash that arced its way into my lap.

"No, no, no. You have to understand. I'm looking for *talent*."

For the next three weeks, Billy would leave the dorm, crunching across the rimy lawns in a straw boater and a candy-striped jacket, twitching his hand like he was conducting an orchestra of frogs, reciting all the parts from *The Importance of Being Earnest* to himself. I never saw him go to class, but by the end of term he had cast the play and got the space—the library and lounge of one of the departments. He'd found a boy, even more handsome than himself, for Jack Worthing; a quiet, overweight girl for Lady Bracknell; two women who, to this day, I'm assuming were paid escorts as Gwendolen and Cecily; a lecturer with a British accent to play Chasuble; and as Miss Prism, a tall, dark-haired sophomore with a face out of a Lewis Carroll photograph, whose name was Merle Kummer.

There were no posters, no announcements, no calls. Somehow, we knew to assemble at 10 p.m. in the College of Letters Lounge. There must have been a hundred of us from the dorms, from classes, from Billy's school in DC, and, too, there was the Hungarian. There was no stage, no curtain, and no furniture. Billy strode into the center of the room, cleared a space, and the play began.

He ate the cucumber sandwiches with an aplomb that showed that he'd been eating them all his life, and when he spoke to Algernon's manservant, Lane, it was with an ease that must have come from living with a household staff. The first act brought out Ernest and Lady Bracknell, and the quiet, overweight girl found her voice behind makeup and costume that had made her unrecognizable to her classmates. We sat, rapt, listening to Algernon on Bunburying—on how his character traveled from city to country, acting out different lies, different personae—and to Ernest revealing that he was Jack in the country, and then to Lady Bracknell, who, upon interrogating Ernest about his having lost his parents, turned to the audience and intoned: "Both? To lose one parent may be regarded as a misfortune—to lose *both* seems like carelessness." We howled, and when Ernest revealed that he was found in a handbag, her incredulous intonation—*a handbag?*—turned this young girl into the very essence of dragonhood.

We couldn't wait through intermission, clamoring for the next act, and then the next. We nodded in our undergraduate self-knowingness as Cecily explained that she could only love someone with the name of Ernest. We held our breath for Jack and Ernest to reveal themselves as one, for Cecily and Gwendolen to fall in love again, for Miss Prism to reveal that it was her bag, that she was writing a three-volume novel, that she was the governess of long ago. *Prism!* Lady Bracknell called, and Merle Kummer sidled across the stage, her face a mask of late-Victorian humiliation, and we all applauded.

The genius of a great performance is to get you to imagine yourself in it. I looked around the room and saw the Chasubles and Prisms, the girls who would grow up into Aunt Augusta, and

I saw how they looked on, mouthing the words of the play, seeing themselves in character. I looked at all the handsome boys, some of them still in prep-school penny loafers and crewneck sweaters, others in denim work shirts and barefoot. I looked at Billy, beaming at his great theatrical success, mugging at the lines and twitching joyously at every laugh. But this was not my play. I thought of you and Mom, playing in *Blithe Spirit, The Rivals, The Odd Couple*; tried hard to see you on the makeshift stage. And I imagined you both, at the play's end, turning as Jack and Gwendolen turn to each other:

JACK: *Gwendolen, it is a terrible thing for a man to find out suddenly that all his life he has been speaking nothing but the truth. Can you forgive me?*

GWENDOLEN: *I can. For I feel that you are sure to change.*

That night, we sat in Billy's room, replaying all the scenes, drinking champagne and smoking cigarettes, and miming all the accents. But when I tried to play, Billy just looked at me. "The line is immaterial," each word transformed from its original into a slight so deep that I thought I would never heal.

My first semester ended in the winter of the oil embargo, and the campus turned down the heat in every building to save money. January intercession had been canceled, spring semester would start late, and we prepared for an unanticipated stretch of six weeks back at home. Some of the boys were going to Florida, or to Europe, but I was getting ready to head back to Pittsburgh, looking for a ride to Bradley Field and the Allegheny Airlines flight. Two nights away, and we were packing up, talking about the aftermath of the Yom Kippur War that autumn. A few of our classmates had left that October, flown to Israel on a day's notice, claimed right of return, and enlisted in the army. At least one was dead. We talked about whether we should have done that, and I looked around at boys whose names were only shards of Jewish selves: Larry, Jon, Mark, Bill; Green, Fink, Ross, Coplon. One of the boys admitted that his parents had been Jewish, but he'd never been Bar Mitzvahed, never studied Torah, didn't even know the prayers. The RA—a blunt senior who had spent the whole fall studying for his LSATs—stood up and announced, "Well then, we'll have to give you a Bar Mitzvah now! Lerer, you're in charge. Get the gear, I'll get the book." The RA banged on everybody's door and woke them up—"Get up, Bar Mitzvah in ten minutes!" I went into the bathroom and dislodged a roll of toilet paper, strung it out and pulled off three foot sections, draped them around everybody's shoulders, and drew blue lines with my ballpoint on the ends. We put on any hat we had—furred ones with ear flaps, an old man's fedora, Billy's straw boater—and at one in the morning we assembled at the head of the dorm's hall, the nineteen-year-old Bar Mitzvah boy, the RA, and me, all in our toilet-paper tallises.

Bar'chu et Adonai hamevorach
Baruch Adonai hamevorach le'olam va'ed
Baruch atah Adonai, Elohenu melech ha'olam,
Asher bachar banu mikol ha'amim
Venatan lanu et torato,
Baruch atah Adonai
Notayn hatorah

Someone pulled out a Bible, and we got the Bar Mitzvah boy to read the passage I had read for my own Bar Mitzvah five years before: the story of how Abram became Abraham, the story of God's covenant with the Jews, the lessons of the circumcision. He read in English and I remembered the Hebrew then as precisely as I remember it now:

V'yehi Avram, ben tishim shana, v'tesha shanim. V'yerah adonai, el Avram, v'yomer elav: Ani el shaddai, hit haleach l'fanai, v'hiyea tamim.

And when Abram was ninety years old and nine, the Lord appeared to Abram, and said unto him, I am the Lord thy God; walk before me and be perfect.

We called each of the boys up for an aliyah, and I renamed all of them: Greenberg and Finkelstein and Rosenbloom and Kaplowitz; Lebel and Yankel and Mendel and Velvel. They doubled over as I blessed them in their toilet-paper tallises and earflaps. By now the noise of celebration had roused the floor above us, where the girls lived, and they came down in their Lanz nightgowns and Dr. Scholl's sandals. One girl, who had grown up in Barbados, ran upstairs and came back down with a couple of bottles of red wine and half a dozen oranges and a wash-bucket, and she poured the wine and cut up the oranges to make sangria, which we passed around and drank in sacramental service. On the sidelines, Billy stood there, in his silk robe and lit cigarette, and when I paused to look him in the eye, he took a drag and said, "I'm told my father was a Jew."

As the ceremony drew to its close and we had made that night another Jewish man, the girls turned to me and said, Sing something Jewish! The sangria bucket was empty and wine-red flecks bled into the blue lines on the tallises, and they turned to me, and even Billy cocked his head. And thinking of the only song I knew, the song you sang on car rides and in restaurants, the song that made us clap along, I sang:

Az der Rebbe Elimelech
Iz gevoren zeyer freylach
Iz gevoren zeyer freylach Elimelech

Hot er oysgeton di tfilen
Un hot ongeton di brilen
Un geschikt nokh di fiddler drey.

I mimed the lines, becoming giddy as I took off my tallis, replaced my glasses, and called at the end: Where are my fiddlers three? Lebel, Yankel, and Mendel turned on their heels and bent their knees and mimed their fiddling, dancing and twitching, and I kept on singing:

Un az di fiddledike fiddlen
Hobn fiddledike fidlen
Hobn fiddledike fidlen hobn zey

And as the snow fell in Connecticut, the cinder-block hall ruptured into one of Chagall's roofs, and green with wash-bucket sangria we danced.

That winter break, I wandered around Pittsburgh, looking into bookstores near the university, driving past my high school haunts. My grades came in the mail: B's all around. Seems that I simply didn't get the purpose of this great books program; seems that I didn't understand just what it meant to "keep a journal" in these classes. Keep a journal, said the Hungarian. Maybe the other kids had gone to schools where the phrase meant something like, write personal, sensitive essays on the books we're reading, type them up, and hand them in, but to me it meant scribble down what you are thinking when you think it. I wrote about *The Importance of Being Earnest* and the Bar Mitzvah. I wrote about how alone I was and how I thought that you were seeing someone else, and what did Mom think. I wrote of how I showered in the evenings in the gym, afraid of running into Billy. I don't know what my teachers made of this, but they seemed as baffled at me as I was with them. It was six weeks before second semester would begin, and all my high school friends were back at their own college campuses by early January. By then, you were off on business trips again, though there was that one evening when you stayed for dinner. Mom made the shrimp dish that I liked and the big salad with the Green Goddess dressing. She was too exhausted to eat. You were, as you reminded us, "cutting back," and my brother, who was fourteen, had spent that year eating nothing but SpaghettiOs. So I was left to eat the whole meal by myself. At one point you looked me right in the eye and said, "Have you thought about a sport?"

A sport? I'd done nothing athletic in high school, managing at one point to get out of senior gym class all together with a doctor's note that Mom had forged. Wesleyan was hardly a sports school—the football team hadn't had a winning season in years, and a bunch of students were petitioning for ultimate Frisbee as a letter-eligible activity. As far as I knew, the only sport that mattered around campus was women's field hockey, and that was largely out of the desire to watch eighteen-year-olds at this newly coed college run around in tartan skirts with sticks. Then there was the crew. I'd seen them in the autumn, rowing on the Connecticut River in the afternoons, curly-haired white boys rippling out of a Thomas Eakins painting.

Sure. I'll sign up for crew.

I called the athletic department and was told that training would begin a week before the term. I packed my books and records and my clothes and got a plane, got Mom to drive me to the airport, and flew to Bradley Field and paid a taxi forty dollars to drive me to Middletown. The dorm was closed up and unheated, but I managed to get let in by a passing janitor. I still had my room key, and I threw my stuff down. Then I thought: I'd never rowed a boat.

The crew was filled with boys who had been rowing since they were thirteen. Kent, Choate, Andover—all the prep schools had teams, and these boys came to it as naturally as I came to complaining. There was no chance of getting in a boat. But the coach looked me up and down and said, "What do you weigh?" I shaved a little off. One-thirty. "Drop ten pounds and you can be the cox of the lightweight boat."

I spent the first weeks of the semester losing weight, talking to students about just what a cox did, and running down whatever I could find about how the shells worked, what an ergometer was, and how I was supposed to steer the boat. I'd hang out in the boat house, looking at the pictures of the crews from past years, all the way back to the 1880s. There were the boys, looking much older than I looked, I thought, in striped jerseys and big mustaches, posing with the oars. Each year the mustaches got smaller, the parts in their hair inched from the middle to the side, and the boys seemed younger, until by the 1920s they were totally clean-shaven, posed in profile with the oars, looking altogether like the casting call for a Noel Coward play.

I bought a sweat suit and wore it constantly, imagining that I could sweat the pounds off. Afternoons, I'd be at the Nautilus, pushing the lead weights with my legs. I skipped lunches, trying to imagine what would help me shed the weight the fastest way possible. One day, I ate nothing but prunes. By mid-February I weighed one twenty-four.

The coxswain is the only person facing forward in a scull. His primary responsibility is to steer the boat. In our shells, there were wires soldered to the rudder, and I held one in each hand, pulling to move the rudder and direct the boat. The cox's job, as well, is to call out the stroke, keep up the pace, and urge the rowers on. A shell's speed is measured in the strokes per minute. Thirty-two is a good clip; thirty-six, and we pulled a wake. To keep the stroke, I had a stopwatch tied with string over my right thigh. The coach taught me to count the strokes over thirty seconds, and then multiply by two. I'd call out, "pull, pull, pull," and with each word the eight boys facing me would pull deep on their oars, then lift them out of the water at the stroke's end, turn them so that the blade shot back flat over the surface, and then turn them back so that they caught the water just below the surface for another pull. The really good oarsmen would know just how deep to set the blade, maximizing pull and minimizing drag. They'd know just how to twist the oar to get the blade up (this was known as feathering). Watching a really good eight, you'd see them seamlessly working as one, pulling and feathering, moving the boat forward in a perfect skim, breathing together.

Mine was not that boat. The boys knew how to row, but they were off in synchrony. The blades dipped unevenly. The feather was low. Once, during practice, one of the boys caught a crab: the blade dipped in the water as he was returning to the start of the stroke, the force of the boat moving forward snapped the whole oar back, and—like Archimedes's lever moving earth—the handle took him in the chest and threw him out of his seat into the water.

Eventually, we learned to pull together, feather high, and sail across the river at a comfortable twenty-eight strokes per minute.

The rowing season was the last eight Saturdays in term. Each of those days, we would get up at 5 a.m. and jog down to the boathouse. Carefully, we'd lift the shells into the trailer, secure them, tie red flags to their tails, which projected three feet beyond the end of the trailer, and then get into a school bus for the drive to the meet—Williams, Amherst, Worcester Polytechnic. By ten o'clock or so, we'd be unloading with all the other schools, getting the shells in the water, trying out the oars, and lubricating the locks. Then the lineup, the call, and the gunshot.

Pull, pull, pull. Take it up to a thirty-two. Feather high.

We lost every race. At one, in Worcester, we were just crossing the halfway mark when the winning boat finished. Because I was the only one facing forward, I was the only one in the boat who could see how far behind we were. Of course, the oarsmen would look back and, seeing no boats behind us, knew we were losing. They just didn't know by how much.

When we raced at Williams, we were nose to nose with one boat, somewhere in the middle of the pack. We couldn't have been more than fifteen feet away, and I was worried that our oars would interlock. We were pulling a thirty-three, and the boys were breathing together, and we matched the stroke of the boat next to us, so close that I could see the brown of the other cox's eyes. And then he looked right at me, turned back to his oarsmen, and yelled, "Take 'em," and with six perfect pulls, they disappeared.

The final meet for the small colleges was the Dad Vail Regatta, held on the Schuylkill River in Philadelphia. It had been going on for nearly forty years and was named for Harry Emerson "Dad" Vail, the coach at Wisconsin. Anyone who raced there simply called it "the Dad." The event was famous for the competitiveness of the rowers, the beauty of the river, and the historic boathouses along the Schuylkill, where the colleges would be hosted. Two days before the race, we loaded up the boats, our clothes, our gear, and drove south out of Middletown, along the turnpike, into the Bronx, across the bridges, down the parkways, and through New Jersey into Philadelphia. The trailer had been loaded up with all four of our boats, each one named for a onetime coach at Wesleyan. My boat, the men's lightweight eight, was the *Garafalo*. We followed in the school bus, making good time at fifty miles an hour. We knew we'd never win, but we talked about the other schools, and famous rowers, and some legendary boats that could, word had it, pull a forty stroke per minute rate throughout a race.

About half an hour north of Philadelphia, someone said, *Look!* And we looked and saw the trailer with the boats fishtailing behind the pickup truck. The restraining pin had obviously come loose. The balance of truck and trailer was off and the whole assembly was weaving back and forth across the highway. We watched in silence as the driver tried to get back in his lane, and then, as he seemed to right himself, the trailer swung out to the right and the tails of the boats, flags flapping in the wind, clipped a telephone pole, which sheared them off like a band saw cutting through balsa. The rear three feet of all four boats went skittering along the shoulder of the highway.

Our bus stopped immediately, and we watched the truck and trailer slow down, finally halting a quarter mile ahead. We got out and saw the shell ends strewn on the shoulder, each one just long enough to show the whole name of its boat. I picked up the *Garafalo*, not knowing what to do with it, and simply held it, realizing that these sweet shells could never be repaired.

I don't remember much after that. I think I recall the coach shooing us back into the bus and getting us to Philadelphia and into a dorm room for the night. The next morning, we toured all the boat clubs on the river, trying to secure replacements for our race. We finally found a club that let us use their boats. They were big, heavy, old things, thick with shellac. We lifted them and strained under their weight. When we got out to practice, the oarlocks creaked. We sat at the dock, watching the racers in the early heats: Massachusetts, La Salle, Marietta. Young men with veins that seemed as thick as my wrist pulled at the drive of each stroke. I had the stopwatch and I timed them: gunshot, then ten strokes that calculated to a forty-two, then settling down into an easy, loping thirty-eight, and then, for the last quarter of the race, a set of strokes that worked out to close to a forty-four. These heats took half the time of our New England races, and I turned to face the eight boys in my lightweight boat, looking at me at that moment, for the first time in the season, hungry for guidance. Men, I said. We're going for form.

I'd never seen them look so good, arms firm, backs supple, eyes closed, pulling together, breathing together, forceful, yet almost serene in the conviction of our loss. Men, I said at the end. Congratulations. In spite of everything, we finished. We looked good. Dad Vail himself would have been proud.

We got back to campus just in time for finals, and two nights later I showed up after dinner at the dorm to find you, just standing there, unannounced, in a blue blazer and deep green tartan wool trousers, with a white shirt and a blue bow tie, your silvering hair swept back down to your collar. You had grown a beard—a mustache and goatee—and the hairs mastered your mouth like the beard Spock wore in that old *Star Trek* episode. Kirk and his companions had been accidentally transported to a parallel universe, a universe in which Starfleet prowls the constellations for booty, where officers advance on the assassination of their superiors, where sex and daggers hug the hips. And there was Mr. Spock, in 1967, with a beard, as if only in a parallel universe would anybody in authority grow such a thing, as if behind that cold, logical face lay an evil self itching to get out. And you, looking part Spock, part Stanislavsky, slimmed down, standing by the pay phone in the hallway, met my eyes like I had just debarked from a destroyer.

You shook my hand in front of everyone—you never, ever shook my hand, always the hugs, the squeezes, the pats on the back—and you came into my room, surveying the white cinder-block walls on which I had placed nothing (I was only there for a year, I said), and took your blazer off, and folded it inside out, carefully creasing its back, and laid it over my desk chair like you were spreading out the ermine. You lay on my bed, in your white shirt and bow tie, stretching yourself out with your hands behind your back, Manet's *Odalisque* right out of Art 101, waiting with the door open for my hallmates to come in and see just who had beamed down.

You were just passing through, coming back from work in Boston to New York. I *had* to come visit. "How about this weekend? Meet me at the St. Regis, the King Cole Room. You know I always stay at the St. Regis."

I know why you loved the place. In the 1970s, the hotel had taken on the patina of stage set, and legend had it that Salvador Dalí and Gala would decamp there for the winter, Dalí every now and then posing in the enormous wing chair by the fireplace, fur-coated, with his signature mustache and walking stick.

That Friday afternoon I found my friend Bob, and we got in his car and drove in early weekend traffic to New York—past the decaying luster of New Haven, past the fronton that had just gone up in Bridgeport for the Caribbean jai alai fans, through Rye and Pelham, over the bridge, and down through the Bronx and Harlem to the hotel. Just leave the car in front, I told Bob. My dad's here, he'll cover it. I had a fiver in my pocket, and I gave it to the bellman as if I were doling out spun gold, and we walked into the hotel lobby—Bob in his jeans and crewneck sweater, and me dressed for the occasion, in a tweed jacket and a paisley bow tie—looking for Dalí and sidling up to the front desk.

Larry Lerer.

I'm sorry, but we've no one by that name here at the hotel.

Lawrence Lerer, then.

No, sir. No Lerer, no Larry, no Lawrence.

"Maybe your dad's travelling under an assumed name?" Bob ventured.

What name? Who else could he be? Did he leave a message, I'm his son.

No, no message here.

I deflated into the big wing chair. I looked at my watch. Miraculously, we'd made it in time. I poked my head into the King Cole Room. No sign of you. I paced. We waited half an hour. Then you showed up, blowing in through the revolving doors, your floor-length raincoat spreading out behind you like a cape. You don't remember any of this.

Where were you, are you staying here, you said the King Cole Room, this is my friend Bob, how's Mom?

And all I can remember now is how you blustered through—well, I thought this would be as good a place to meet as any; yes, I was here for a while but I'm staying with a friend; I don't see what the problem is, you're here, I'm here, Bob (if that is his *real* name) is here, let's go.

Bob looked at me as if to say, I bet this happens all the time, and we walked through the lobby.

I thought we were going to eat at the King Cole Room, I said, but you just looked incredulously at me.

The focal point of the King Cole Room was a mural by Maxfield Parrish that rendered the king and his court with saturated colors and exaggerated beauties. I'd spent the drive telling Bob all about it, and I reminded him of the sangria Bar Mitzvah, when I sang the "Rebbe Elimelech," a Yiddish version of "Old King Cole," with his fiddlers three and his spectacles and his tefillin.

But we were out the door, in a cab (what about Bob's car?), and off to Pearl's in Midtown. Offering overpriced, watered-down Chinese food, it was the restaurant of the moment, the walls completely black, the table settings black, with brilliant white chopsticks set against them like chalk on blackboard. Of course, we had no reservation, and the place was almost full, but you had a gift for intimidating ethnic waiters, and after a few minutes of Stalinesque diplomacy—what do you mean that table is reserved? I see no one there? We'll be out in an hour!—we were seated.

No menus, you said, as you brushed away the waiter. We'll have the minced squab in lettuce leaves, the lemon chicken, the tangerine beef, and the eggplant. Rice all around. I'll have a Lillet. Men? We ordered a couple of beers.

Your Lillet came, the color of liquid straw. It's a wonderful drink, you said (a year or so later, I ordered it at a restaurant and the waiter brought it to my date, correcting himself on my prompting with an exaggerated "Sorry, *sir*"). Bob drank his beer like it was the only thing between him and an invading army, and I knew, as he must have known, at that very moment, why you brought us here. You said nothing. You didn't have to. We looked around at the skinny men and the skinnier women. We stared as the servile waiters took back dishes that the other diners didn't like. We watched as the minced squab came and you carefully laid it out in the lettuce leaves, mounding and shaping it into a little sausage, and then rolling the whole assembly up into a lettuce tube and opening your mouth and eagerly putting it in. We watched as you held up the chopsticks and asked for a fork ("chopsticks are such an affectation," you pronounced). I liked the lemon chicken—deep-fried breast strips covered in a tart syrup—but the tangerine beef was stringy and the eggplant mushy. You ate none of your rice ("I'm cutting back"), and even before Bob and I were done you pushed your chair back and lit up a cigarette, took a deep drag, closed one eye, and looked at me.

"That's some tie."

You took a sniff and threw out your left hand like you were conducting an orchestra, but only to pull back the sleeve and check your watch. With the same hand, you snapped your fingers and the waiter brought the check, and you pulled out a wad of twenties and put six of them down without even looking at the bill. Well, men, it's been a joy, and you got up and threw your coat over your shoulders without putting your arms in the sleeves and stepped out into the Midtown night. And Bob said, "You think I could finish his rice?" We sat there without saying a word, left the restaurant and walked back to the St. Regis where, surprisingly, Bob's car was still in front, and we got in and drove the two hours back to Middletown.

That spring, the magnolias and the dogwoods opened late, and by the time exams were over, they were just past prime, the pink-edged petals falling like autumn leaves from last November. The literature teacher had made us read the whole of Joyce's *Ulysses*, referring in class to chapter titles that I didn't know existed (where in the book does it say, "Oxen of the Sun"?), and all I got out of the class was his announcement: "Leopold Bloom's real name was Virag, which is Hungarian for flower." I never found a girl to sleep with me, while Bob, I later learned, was famous around campus for having gotten laid within an hour of the first day's freshman orientation. I never went back to the boathouse. I vowed to get the best grades that I could, cash in my AP high school credits, and finish in three years. I went back to my old fascinations—Anglo-Saxon, *Beowulf*—decided I would be an English major, go to grad school, teach. I'd keep a journal of the books I'd read. I'd never learn Hungarian or change my name. And I would never ask you if you spoke the truth. Can you forgive me?

The last day of freshman year I packed my books and my records, my stereo and my electric typewriter, and I put on my tweed jacket, even though it was May and humid in the Connecticut valley. I'd asked Bob to take me to the airport, even though it was precisely in the opposite direction from his home in Pelham, but he said he'd drive me anyway. We were leaving the dorm when Billy came out holding his straw boater.

"Listen man, I haven't lived at home since I was thirteen. You'll do fine. Consider yourself lucky. I never really knew my father."

And then he gave me his hat and walked away.

SIX

Iceland

I left the restaurant and walked back to his apartment in the rain. He had been dead two days and, still, I couldn't get Mom on the phone. I had called a friend of hers. No answer. I had called my brother. "Oh, she's fine." Find her, I barked. Finally, that night, I got ahold of her. She had turned the ringer down on the phone one evening and forgotten to bring it back up.

He's gone.

"Thank God. What a relief for all of us. You know it's a blessing that boy of yours won't have to grow up with him. He never cared about anyone other than himself. Don't fool yourself. He never really loved you. You were his pet."

His pet. I tried to think of anything that would confound her: remember Brooklyn, and the trips to Jack's and the museum; remember how he let me grow those strawberries, or how he bought that great big house for us, or how he took us all to Europe?

But all that vanished, and all I could think of was one morning during winter break, my senior year in college. I was lying in bed in the big stone house in Pittsburgh, when I heard him on the phone.

"He wants to make a career out of Old English. Can you believe that? He wants to go to Oxford. We took him there when we were all in Europe—you remember, he was fifteen—and I guess he never got over it. He's applied for a Rhodes Scholarship. Of course, we don't think he'll get it."

I didn't. I got a Keasbey Scholarship instead. Funded by the largesse of a Philadelphia widow, the Keasbey was available to students from the northeast colleges and universities. A kind of baby Rhodes, they called it, and after an interview with four sad lawyers in blue suits, I got a phone call in the dead of winter telling me I'd been awarded the scholarship and I was going to Hertford College, Oxford, to study English philology.

"Philology" means love of language, but for a college student of the 1970s it was much less a case of love than of fantasy. J. R. R. Tolkien was a philologist: a scholar of Old and Middle English, of Old Norse and Old Welsh, of dialects and diphthongs. *The Hobbit* and *The Lord of the Rings* were grounded in his linguistic play. Runes scattered across pages; etymologies danced in the dialogue. Old Bilbo Baggins of Bag End meant nothing more than Bilbo of the *cul de sac*—as if Tolkien had looked back at nine centuries of French incursion in the British Isles, only to retranslate English life back into Anglo-Saxon; as if he could, with a stroke of his philology, undo the Norman Conquest.

I read *Beowulf* in junior high. I had been exiled to the library for some infraction (probably passing love notes in math class), and I pulled a copy off a shelf, attracted by the glittering cover. It was really a children's edition, but it had amazing illustrations: Grendel strode across the pages, dripping with blood, his skin an electric green. He walked across the misty slopes, over the moorlands, bearing God's ire. I remembered how the names, even in the children's prose translation, sounded like incantations: Wealhtheow, Hrothgar, Unferth. The translation also gave the flavor of the Anglo-Saxon, with its short, monosyllabic words and its attempts at alliteration. A few years later, in high school, we read the Burton Raffel translation, and I then trooped off to the Carnegie Library in Pittsburgh to get a copy of a facing page,

Anglo-Saxon/modern English edition. I sat up nights reading the text aloud, trying to get a feel for the language and the phrasing. Kennings—those noun metaphors—gripped me: "road of the whale" was the sea; "God's candle" was the sun.

The old Germanic words reminded me of my parents' Yiddish. The prefix for the participle in the Germanic languages is *ge-*. In Old English, *geworhton* meant "built"; *gesceawod* meant "had gazed upon." I listened to recordings made by Helge Kökeritz, the Swedish-born Yale professor, as he intoned *Beowulf* in something like a blend of bardic thrill and Scandinavian frost: "Geworhton ða Wedra leode, helo on hoe, se waes heah and brad." Then the people of the Weder-Geats built a mound on the hillside, it was high and broad. And later, Beowulf's funeral pyre, built in ten days (*betimbredon on tyn dagum*). I danced to the alliterations, tripped my feet over the meter. I turned to Grendel, marking his way along the moorlands. I found his mother, *gemyndig*, mindful, remembering, harboring a grudge. I saw the fractured bodies of the Danes and thought of Mom's *gehacktet tsuris*, hacked up troubles.

The September after college, I raided Brooks Brothers for tweeds and flannels, packed my books in steamer trunks, and spent seven days on the Queen Elizabeth II sailing from New York to Southampton. This was the ship the Rhodes boys sailed on, and I quickly was excluded from the group. Not one of us, where did you say you went to college, what were you planning to "read" when you "went up"? No one had heard of the Keasbey, and for these tall young men off to read Philosophy and Politics and Economics at Christ Church and St. Johns, a boy in tweeds planning on doing philology at Hertford was met with as much distaste as if I made them watch me put ketchup on peanut butter and banana sandwiches.

Hertford. It was little college, famous for its replica of Venice's Bridge of Sighs, for the fact that Evelyn Waugh had been there in the 1920s, and for its execrable food. A story that I heard within a day of arriving was that, as a joke, some students had inserted tiny half-pence pieces in their uneaten Brussels sprouts and left the plates to be cleared by the staff, and then three days later one of the college tutors bit into a half-pence piece at high table dinner. I was assigned a two-room suite furnished with couches of Waugh's vintage, a "scout" who would make the bed, and a tutor, who left our first meeting halfway through, realizing he was out of cigarettes, stunning me to silence with his slang: "Sorry, must pop out for a fag."

I found a group of Americans from New College who had clustered, as a kind of court, around a boy I'd gone to college with (but didn't know), who grew up on the Upper East Side of Manhattan and, as his first activity on arriving in England, bought a Triumph TR-7 convertible and drove it right up to the college gates to unpack. He hosted parties in his rooms: cheeses and wines I'd never heard of, pipes and cigars. One side of his family had been in the wine business in Europe before the war, and he knew his bottles better than I knew Old English. He taught me to look for key terms on the labels: "mise en bouteille au chateau." A cru bourgeois, he noted, can sometimes be just as good as a premier cru, and for half the price. One evening, he set up a raclette table in the common room: a half a wheel of cheese sat in front of the fireplace, just close enough to let the open cut warm into softness. Slices of firmly boiled potatoes stacked themselves on plates. He showed us how to take each slice, run it along the soft side of the cheese, and bring it to our mouths just as it cooled. I watched him perform, and as the cheese strung out in spider strands he opened his mouth and popped the whole thing in, like Grendel gobbling a Dane.

In my prewar rooms, I read the *Ormulum* and the Orthoepists (a group of seventeenth-century scholars who invented systems of phonetic transcription), memorized sound changes from Germanic to Old English, and translated *Gawain and the Green Knight*.

The Oxford of the 1970s had an elegiac quality about it. J. R. R. Tolkien and W. H. Auden had both died within two years of my arrival, and Oxford mourned them with a gowned theatrics that could barely compensate for the indifference it had had to them when they were living. Tolkien: medieval, fantastic, inward-looking. Auden: emotive, modern, all too real. They were the two poles of the university, and my tutors were their students and their self-appointed heirs. One of them did her thesis under Tolkien in the 1950s, and one day midway through my first year, she asked me what my first name was. It's Seth. "Oh, that's your first name? I thought your surname was Seth-Lerer and I always wondered what a Christian name would be before that." Another tutor could not have been more than thirty-five but had the affect of an aged heiress from an Agatha Christie novel. Her first words to me in our tutorial on Middle English dialects were, "Do you know your don?" My don? I thought you were my don, recalling, proudly, that the word "don" came from Latin *dominum*, by way of Spanish *Don*, and was the Oxford colloquialism for a college tutor. "No, no, I mean Richard Your Don, author of the *Handbook of Middle English Grammar*." Oh, Richard Jordan, the German philologist whose *Handbuch der mittelenglishen Grammatik* of 1925 had appeared in an English translation in the early 1970s. "Yes. Your Don."

I joined a group of student poets who seemed thrilled to have an energetic young American among their ranks. We talked about the writers that we loved in ugly pubs, and we agreed to meet every Tuesday, in one of the college lounges, to share our work. At the first meeting, we went around the room and everybody read their poems. There were elegies for unborn sisters, paeans to dogs, some fractured lyrics, and then me. I read a poem I had written on the death of Robert Lowell, and made much of the fact that it had been accepted by the *Sewanee Review* for publication that spring. I went through the poem, analyzing all the references, making a claim for formal verse, and talking about Lowell's impact on my life—his early iambic pentameters, his mania, his stance against the war. The next Tuesday I showed up at the lounge. Nobody else was there.

They were all there that spring, though, when Ted Hughes came to read. Hughes: leathern, drunk, unshaven, with that "I killed her" look on his face. He read the "Crow" poems without looking up, hunched over the hill of his sorrow, playing the wounded poet to the hilt.

He'd brought along a poet I'd not heard of yet, Seamus Heaney, who had begun his career writing dazzling jewels of verse about Northern Ireland and his literary calling and had, in the mid-1970s, turned to poems about bog people. These were men and women, some dead on their own, some murdered horribly, who had been preserved in peat in northern Europe for something like fifteen hundred years and then were dug up, with their skin tanned like leather and their teeth like burnished ivory. After Hughes hauled himself offstage, Heaney got up, red faced and smiling, and read "The Tollund Man":

> Some day I will go to Aarhus
> To see his peat-brown head,
> The mild pods of his eye-lids,
> His pointed skin cap.

He went on, evoking the old alliterations of Germanic verse, alluding to the buried dead like markers of old nations, refracting his sense of longing through his Northern Irish lilt, looking for "Something of his sad freedom."

That term, I was beginning Old Norse with the Tolkien student, and I ran to her the next day: help me be Seamus Heaney; send me to Iceland to find the Norse dead; help me translate the sagas and the Eddas; let me live in their Middle Earth. She wrote off, made a few phone calls, and by late May it was all arranged. I'd fly to Reykjavik and stay with Jonas Kristjansson, the keeper of the institute where all the Old Norse manuscripts were held, the most important scholar of Icelandic literature and culture, and he'd set me up with a farm family where I would work throughout the summer and learn modern Icelandic—so close to Old Norse, I was told, that even rustic shepherds could read *Njáls Saga*.

I studied frantically, took a tutorial in modern Icelandic with a graduate student, read newspapers and books, and prepared the set texts for what would be my course of exams the following year. These included the mythological writings of Snorri Sturlusson, a thirteenth-century Icelandic bishop who codified all the old tales of the gods and heroes, together with a treatise on poetry; the poems of the oldest Norse peoples, tales of Hamthir, Atilla, Brunhild; and the saga of Hrafnkel, a bullying landowner from the earliest days of Iceland's settlement, whose story was written in a prose simple enough even for me. I packed my books, blue jeans, sweaters, my Icelandic dictionary, pencils, and a writing pad, and on July Fourth I took a plane from Gatwick to Glasgow and then from Glasgow to Reykjavik.

"Reykjavik" literally means the reeking seaport, a name conjured from the mists and sulfurous miasma that hung over the cove, the legacy of centuries of geothermal bubbling and of cold air coming off glaciers and settling, wet and heavy, over the warmer sea. I landed at the airport on a runway that looked adzed out of lava, took a bus to the terminal downtown, and waited for the Kristjanssons. I should say Jonas, for as I learned on the plane, Icelanders should be called only by the first names. The phone book, even, was arranged by first names, with the patronymics afterward and, sometimes, an appellation of a job (Jon Jonsson, baker). There were no inherited last names, just first names and father's names, and I thought how I'd introduce myself: Seth Lawrensson, Seth Larsson. *Komiþ þjer saelir,* I memorized—may bliss come to you, the standard greeting of hello.

I waited four hours. There were no phones, no messages. Icelanders, the woman at the information desk informed me, have complicated lives. They'll be here.

Jonas did show up, oblivious to the time, completely unaware that I had landed half a day before and sat, the lone green-eyed Jew on the entire island, for hours in a terminal of brown-eyed blonds. He spoke to me right away in Icelandic, and I couldn't understand a word. I beg your pardon. "Oh, you don't speak Icelandic?" Well, I was studying it at Oxford, I began, and I reeled off some of the stuff I'd memorized and said something like, everyone says the language hasn't changed in a thousand years. "Oh that!" He laughed. "No one really believes that. " He drove me to his house (by now, it was close to midnight), where I did manage to meet his wife and ask her for a glass of water—*latið mik fá glas vatn.* I went to bed not having eaten in a day. The next morning I woke up, no one in the house. I took a bath—*Ég vil að baða mík.* I'd figured out the request, but there was no one there to ask. I got dressed, found no food in the house, and walked out into Reykjavik, looking for something to eat and something to do.

Three days passed like that. Each evening I'd come back, the door would be open, someone might or might not be home. Then, on the fourth day, Jonas announced he was taking me to the bus, that I should tell the driver I was going to Uppsalir, a farm in the north, and he'd let me off. About how long is the ride, I asked. Oh, about ten hours.

There was, or seemed to be, only one major highway round the island. The bus snaked across lava plains and fjords, through headlands, into misty valleys. Half-sleeping, half-carsick, I heard the alliterations in the rumble of the engine.

Đa com of more, ofer misthleoþu
Grendel gongan, Goddes ire baer.

It was day's end when the bus stopped, dead in the middle of the road, and let me out. Uppsalir. I got out, he drove off, and even though it was past ten o'clock, the sun was bright in the Icelandic summer sky. *Godes condel beorht.*

On the western horizon, a dust cloud came up, moving fast, like (I remembered) Robby the Robot tooling along the desert in *Forbidden Planet*, while the astronauts gaped in mute wonder at his speed. A jeep pulled up, and a young man, about my own age, with snowy blond hair halfway down his back, jumped out. He stuck out his hand and said his name, Eythor, and I said Seth, and we got in and drove across the plains, up to the hillside, where a little farmhouse stood, where I would work and sleep and eat for the next eight weeks without a sunset.

We parked and walked into the house, warm with the smell of geothermal heat (all the hot water, I was told later, came from the local hot springs, and the whole house smelled like a burnt match). I met, first, the father, Arni, whom I'd meet again the next day when he took me out to fix a fence and twisted the barbed wire with his bare hands. I met Solveg, the mother, who made cakes and cookies without measuring a thing. I met Drifa, the elder daughter, and her boyfriend, Vigfuss, who promised to show me how to shear a sheep with nothing but a pair of scissors. And then there was Anna-Solveg.

Anna-Solveg, thirteen, towheaded, spoke some English, smart. She had the same garnet-brown eyes as everybody in the family, and she wore a torn rag around her neck with as much panache as if it were an Hèrmes scarf.

Love at first sight. It was her room they'd put me in, much to her anger, and her anger made her even more compelling. She had learned her English, as she told me, not only from school, but from listening to ABBA records, and hardly a day went by when she did not break into a song from one of their albums — lyrics syrupy with Scandinavian imaginings of American popular culture, songs she had clearly memorized phonetically, with no idea of what they meant:

> *You're a teaser, you turn 'em on*
> *Leave them burning and then you're gone*
> *Looking out for another, anyone will do*
> *You're in the mood for a dance*
> *And when you get the chance . . .*
> *You are the dancing queen . . .*

She took me to the shed that first morning, with her mother, to introduce me to the cows. Each one had a name, but I can only recall one now. *Midnaetti,* Midnight, they called her, black as the night sky that I would never see, uddered each morning with milk that Anna-Solveg would squeeze out, working each teat like she was wringing solace from a stone.

I was given a shovel. *Moka skít,* she said, and I could figure out the etymologies—*moka,* to muck; *skít,* shit. I shoveled cow-shit for an hour, piled it into loads outside the barn, where it matured into manure. Now, lead them up the mountain, she said. She gave me a long stick and showed me how to hit each one on the rear to get them moving, how to say "hloot, hloot" to prod them along, and then she pointed up the hill, an hour's walk. I pushed them on, covered in cow dung, along the fence line, and an hour later I stood looking down at Uppsalir, the river mouth that lead out to the fjord, the snow against the opposite hillside.

By ten o'clock, I was back in the house, having coffee and bits of herring on black bread, brushing the flies off my dungy jeans, when an old man walked into the kitchen. He was no taller than I was, but he carried himself as if, with a word, he could stretch up to ceiling height. A face fjorded with wrinkles, blond hair turned waxen gray, and eyes as brown as garnets. *Komið þjer saelir,* I said, smiling and putting out my hand. He looked at me and simply said yes, *Já,* the way some Icelanders did, sucking in the word rather than breathing it out—*Já,* pronounced "yeow," sucked in like the breeze in a cave mouth, a word that came to me at that moment as an acknowledgment not of my presence but of life itself.

This was Bjarni, Arni's father, then eighty-six years old, who'd built the farm and lived until the 1960s in a sod hut on the property, who—I was told that evening when I was formally introduced, or better yet, presented, to him—would eat only from the wedding silver and china that he'd received sixty years before, and that I had the special task of setting for him at the evening meal. Each word he uttered came out like an oracle. I don't recall him ever speaking an entire sentence. Every now and then, he'd suck in a significant "Já," or comment on weather or the landscape:

þokk (mist)

Snjá (snow)

Rigna (rain)

Hraun (lava)

One day, I pieced together a sentence about a sheep I'd seen high up the mountain when I'd led the cows. The sheep was dead, its entrails splayed across its wool, bite marks across its throat. All I could say was, *Ég sá kindur sem var dauður.* He looked at me, breathed in a "Já," and smiled, as if to recognize that I could speak, that I had understood farm life and death, that I could see in that dead animal the way things were up here.

On Sundays, we would visit relatives and friends, and they would introduce me as their American student. *Ég er námsmaðr,* I'd announce. I am a student. *Ég elska Islands.* I love Iceland. I'd look around these afternoons, at all the boys flirting with Anna-Solveg, and her laughter, and her towhead and her eyes as brown as garnets, and she'd look at me across the room and jerk her chin away like a shying horse, and turn her back on me. *Ég elska þig*. I practiced it silently.

What does your father do, the relatives would always ask, and I would try to explain: he's a management consultant; he was a teacher; he's an amateur actor. None of these phrases translated. An uncle peered at me one afternoon, and said the word *Menntamálaraðuneytið*, and I nodded. I looked it up later: it means ministry of education. Sure. From then on, I told people that my father worked in the ministry of education, and they'd nod, size me up and down, and then say that they'd never seen anyone with green eyes before.

One Sunday, in an unexpected burst of summer warmth, we all went swimming. Ninety kilometers away, there was a public pool, fed from a local hotsprings, and I knew that we were getting close when the rich sulfur smell blew in through the jeep's open windows. I had no bathing suit. Vigfuss found a pair of my blue jeans, took them outside, and cut the legs off, and proudly presented them to me, like a cat proud of a dead bird at the doorway: bathing suit, he said, in English.

The men changed in a large, communal open space, barred only by a wooden door, no roof, no lockers, a few benches, and a toilet. All the men stripped down and I noticed just then that they all were uncircumcised. I don't think I'd ever seen an uncircumcised penis before, and here were dozens of them, tufted in dark blond hair, their heads cowled in their foreskins. Even the non-Jews of my generation had been circumcised back home, and here were naked men, walking around without the slightest care, each foreskin pointing at me like an accusation. There was no wall to hide behind, no locker door, no bush. I pulled my pants down, took off my underwear, and stood there, two breaths, three breaths, waiting for someone to notice, wondering if they'd point. *Ég er Gyðyingur*, I am a Jew. I'd practiced that sentence for just such a moment, but nobody seemed to notice, no one cared. *Umskorrin*, circumcised. I knew that word as well.

This was the genius of Icelandic, a language without loanwords. For a thousand years, the Icelanders would make up words for unfamiliar things out of their own vocabulary. Great polysyllables for science or technology or faith would be reduced to what my tutor said were calques: words made up, bit by bit, by translating the parts of other words. The television, for example, was the *sjón-varp*, the picture thrower; the radio, the *utvarp*, the out-thrower, a calque for transmitter. *Umskorrin* meant "scored around," and I looked down at my Jewishness and saw it, scored around, the ceremony of the English word now stripped down to a scar.

I put my cutoffs on and ran out to the pool. The water smelled like rotten eggs, but I jumped in, and it was hot—not just warm, but really hot, like a fresh-drawn bath. I flailed around, feeling myself poach in the water, and Anna-Solveg came up, wearing nothing but a pair of cutoffs herself and a bra, and said, "þu ert moðirsik," and splashed me as she swam away. *Moðirsik*, home-sick I thought, sick for my mother, though what at this moment would lead Anna-Solveg to such insight into my loneliness I could not fathom.

When we got back to the farm, I looked up *moðirsik* in my dictionary. It means hysterical. Hysterical—from *hystero*, the Greek for uterus, for in the nineteenth century the physiologists who coined the term thought that the uterus itself was mobile, strange, and full of vapors, and any woman who behaved in strange ways was thought to be suffering from such disturbance. *Moðirsik*, unmanned, with a dictionary on Anna-Solveg's bed.

That night, Eythor took me out to the barn and pointed to a great rolled-up net. He motioned for me to grab one end, and he took the other, and we walked down to the river that led to the fjord. I held one side against the river bank and he walked across, waist deep, without flinching, unrolling the net across the current, staking it on the other bank, four hundred or so feet away. Then he tromped back across the riverbed, clapped me on the back, and said, "Á morgun við bordum fisk," tomorrow we eat fish.

And sure enough, he woke me up before I had to go and shovel shit the next morning, and we grabbed the net, now heavy and twitching, and half a dozen fish—part trout, part salmon, so they seemed—were caught gill-wise across the webbing. *Silungur*, he called them. We dislodged them, banged their heads against the rocks, and brought them to the house. That night, poached in home-churned butter from the cows I'd harried, with potatoes dug from the backyard, rhubarb and yogurt for dessert, they went down, pink-fleshed and perfect.

In his *Saga*, Hrafnkel takes on a young boy as a farmhand. He can do anything he wants, but he can never ride Hrafnkel's favorite horse, Freyfaxi. Do that, and I'll kill you. But one day, the boy finds that the sheep have scattered, and he goes to get a horse to chase them. Only one remains for him to mount, Freyfaxi. He gets on, rides off, collects the sheep, and then comes back. Freyfaxi gallops up to the farmstead, and Hrafnkel comes out, finding the horse all sweaty. Did you ride him? he says to the boy. And the boy does not deny it. Hrafnkel takes his axe and kills the boy with a single blow.

The story goes on, with the relatives pressing a lawsuit, getting compensation, punishing the farmer. But pride intervenes, and all the men eventually get their comeuppance. Everyone gets an option: do this and you'll live; do that and you'll die. You have two choices—*Mun ek bjoda þér tvá kosti*. The phrase shows up again and again. There's very little in the story of great drama. I'd sit in Anna-Solveg's room, reading the story, writing down vocabulary, translating and trying to make sense of its simplicity. There were no gods or heroes. There was no great drama, like the burning of

Njál's house or the performance of Egil's poetry. Just a few men of few words, and a horse, and choices.

Literature is the story of bad choices. If the boy had not ridden the horse, there would be no story. If the men had not gone after Hrafnkel afterward, there would be no story. If Hrafnkel had not sought revenge, there would be no story. Good choices make for quiet lives. Bad choices make for saga. Had I stayed at home, there'd be no story.

I was not made for saga. Each day, I'd try a task they'd set me: little ones at first, like shoveling shit or digging up potatoes. The greater challenges eluded me. One morning, Midnight pushed me against the barbed wire as I tried to get her up the hill, and Arni had to come, a smile as wide as the river mouth across his face, to disentangle me like a trapped trout. Another day, I went off with Eythor to find huge driftwood logs along the seacoast. There were no trees here—they had all been cut down by settlers hundreds of years before, and nothing grew back, just scrub and grass, and lava. But the farmers knew that far across the North Sea into Norway, loggers bundled their haul into great rafts and floated them along the coast to shipping ports, and every now and then, a log or two might dislodge itself from the pack and float along the currents, lodging, months later, against sandbars on the northern coast of Iceland. We took the jeep and spun along the beach, kicking up surf and sand with the rear tires, until we spied one, bleached out, like a beached sea creature. It must have been twenty feet long, and I thought only of Beowulf's ocean—*hron-rad*, the road of the whale. We managed to roll it up-beach, lift it up onto the jeep's roof, and tie it on. We drove back, celebrating our dead catch, as if we had speared a monster.

That evening, Arni, Eythor, and some local men dragged the log up the hill to what would be the new barn. This was, now I understood, to be the central post for a new roof, and I was given a shovel again, this time to dig a hole for the log. It had started to drizzle, and the dirt turned quickly into earth-shit, but I dug away, until after an hour or so I had made a hole about three feet deep. Arni and the men lifted the log upright and stuck it in the hole. It quivered, but it held. While all hands held it straight, Eythor then came up with a wheelbarrow full of cement. He dumped it in, much of it splattering on my boots, and then tamped it down. We stood there, holding up the log, the rain now pelting, all sense of clock-time lost, until the cement set enough for us to go inside for dinner.

Days passed. The barn took shape around the log, wall studs and bracers and then corrugated steel sheets that Arni had can- nibalized from a neighbor, nail-pounded into wood frames, and finally plans for a great roof that would peak just at the log's top. Eythor sighted along the wall rim, and he said something to Arni, who said something to Anna-Solveg, who translated.

The log is six inches too high. You'll have to climb up and cut off six inches from the top. Here's the saw. And she walked away.

I stood there, surrounded by people I had never seen—not just the family, but strange men in boots and sweaters, one smoking a pipe, another shoving snuff up his nose, men with deep blond hair and dark brown eyes, whose faces hadn't laughed in generations, men so quietly strong that the rain didn't even dare wet them, and there I was, soaked to the skin, realizing at that moment that my presence on the farm was news for miles around—that everyone was there to watch me climb the log and cut the top off, in the rain, to see if they could laugh again.

And the American, green-eyed, dripping wet, slung the bow saw over his shoulder like a real bow, and, finding the still re- maining nubs and knots along the log, shimmied up the sixteen feet or so until he reached the top. Then, bracing my legs around the log, I took the saw and began to work. Six inches from the top. I pulled the blade against the wood, and heard the snoring sound of cutting, and the log shook, and I closed my eyes and sawed away, slaying this dragon as the men watched and nobody breathed. After what seemed a lifetime, the top disk of wood sloughed off, and I slid down, my inner thighs now stuck with splinters. I turned to them, waiting for applause, or laughter, or a slap on the back, or a thank-you.

Já.

Weeks went by, and the summer chilled. The sun began to skirt the horizon, and we were all outside now, sixteen hours a day, cutting the hay and raking it and baling it and stacking it in the silo. During the winter, when the cows were housed inside the shed and the sheep huddled on the hillside, they would eat the hay we'd cut and baled. By late August, the fishing nets were coming up empty, and Eythor and I drove off to the communal freezer in the town for food.

There was no cash at Uppsalir. The lambs' meat and the wool would be exchanged for credits in the town, and Arni's family would buy their fuel, supplies, and food against the credit of their crop. All of the local farmers kept their meat in a warehouse freezer. Great cabinets, smoking with dry ice, lined the walls. Eythor took a key out of his pocket, turned it in the padlock, and we walked in. Everywhere there were sheep's heads, blackened with freezer burn. That's all that's left, he said, explaining that after the autumn slaughter, the freezer would fill again with fleshy haunches. For now, all we had were the heads. He grabbed a plastic bucket and plucked a few of them, weighing them like melons (if he'd ever seen a melon), gauging their quality by their heft in his hands. They would defrost by the time we returned to Uppsalir, and Solveg would boil them down, letting the bits and pieces of flesh fall from the cheeks, then picking it and shredding it and mixing it with onions and potatoes for a stew.

One day, about a week before I left, they'd either run out of sheeps' heads or tired of the meat, and Eythor came in with a bucket of frozen blackness. It was about half full, with the middle raised up in a hump caused by the freezing, and I looked down, seeing flecks of white and little grains, wondering if we now were eating dirt.

It was sheep's blood, and it was Drifa's job to cook it. *Drifa,* "snow drift," I thought, as she put her snowy hands into the thick, coagulated mess, palmed it by gobs into a pot, and heated it on the stove. She stirred in oatmeal, milk, a little salt and sugar, and it bubbled and popped. She let it cool, then spooned it into cheesecloth bags, tied them up, and let them dry. That night, she took the bags, now looking like bloodied mozzarella cheese, and put them in a pot of boiling water, poaching them out. She served them up, sliced into rings, with boiled potatoes. I bit in, surprised at how grainy the blood sausages were, gritty against my teeth. The family ate in silence.

Last meals, last chores. I said good-bye to Midnight, packed my things, and took a bath. I dressed, and found Solveg in the kitchen. All the men and the girls were in the fields, but they wanted me to know how much they liked me and how much they wished me well. Then she reached into her vast knitting bag and pulled out a turtleneck sweater. She had been knitting it the whole time I was there, just for me. It had white bands and brown bands across it, not dyed but the natural color of the wool. There were no seams, as she had knitted it on circular needles, making, in effect, great tubes of wool. I put my bags down, took the sweater, and pulled it on. It fit perfectly. How did you know my size, I asked, in English, and whether or not she understood me she put her palms flat against my chest and then against my sides and said, also in English, "I looked." And then she kissed me, and I took the bus ten hours back to Reykjavik, to stay with Jonas one more day, then fly back to New York and then to Pittsburgh before going back to Oxford in September.

The second year at Oxford, I did little else but dream. *Mig dreymði,* I dreamed. The verb is a reflexive one, with the subject only implied. *Mig dreymði,* literally, "it dreamed to me." I'd fall asleep across my 1930s divan, or on chairs in the Bodleian Library, feeling the scratch of Solveg's undyed wool around my neck. And it would dream to me of Anna-Solveg and her petulance, of Drifa and the blood sausages. I'd silently mouth all the sentences I'd memorized:

Ég er námsmaðr
Ég er Gyðyingur
Ég elska Islands
Ég elska þig

And when I could not sleep, I'd walk across the colleges to where my rich friend lived, and I would entertain his courtiers like a *skald.* I'd wear my sweater, and I'd tell them all about the phone that was so old you had to crank it up and call up Central, about the little horse I'd learned to ride, about the driftwood, about the rain, about the hay, and about Anna-Solveg, and when the mood was right, I'd climb the roof-beam and mime sawing the end.

SEVEN

Upriver

I was still sitting at his desk, the phone down, his Ghurka address book still lying nearby. I thought of calling Mom back, thought of everything, but then got up and looked around. Pictures were everywhere. He'd carefully framed sepias of his mother and his aunts, his father at a table playing poker with a cousin. And then the pictures of himself: at two, bundled in a woolen hat and scarf; at five, in short pants and a Buster Brown haircut; at thirteen, in the tallis and the yarmulke of the Bar Mitzvah; and then in the army, with his relatives, with me, with my brother, with my wife and son. There was no picture taken after 1925 that didn't have him in it, and I picked them up from side tables and countertops, turning them in my hands like they were stelae from a tomb. I found my own Bar Mitzvah picture, and then drawers of photo albums: Dad and me at my college graduation; Dad and me in the courtyard of my Oxford college; Dad and me in Chicago, when I got my PhD; and Dad at my wedding, with a sheaf of flowers in one hand, his other hand spread out, and his mouth caught in midlaugh, as if to say, can you believe he found *her*?

I had.

We met on the first day of graduate school. I was sitting in the lounge at Harper Hall when she came in with boxes of books, a small TV set, and a carton of kitchenware. I held the elevator for her, peering into the splitting carton to see knives and forks, plates, a few pans, and a corkscrew. Later that afternoon, I walked by her open door to find her neatly setting books along the only shelf provided: Derrida's *De la grammatologie*, the Romances of Chrétien de Troyes, a set of French plays, and a large, yellow hardback of Hans Küng's *On Being a Christian*.

Hey.

Hey.

I walked in without being asked and went over to the bookshelf. As she unpacked, I fingered the spines, moving from top to bottom of the English books and from bottom to top along the French. I pulled down the Küng, and opened it at random.

The author will reject no suggestion which may help to make his meaning clear. To this extent all doors remain open to greater truth.

"You into Jesus?" I ventured.

"Oh, I've just been doing a lot of thinking."

Me, too, I said, and didn't see her for a week.

That first weekend of school, one of the older graduate students in the dorm suggested that we all go to the top of the John Hancock Building downtown. There was a bar on the ninety-fifth floor, and he got it in his head that we'd all drive in to the city, take the elevator up, and drink till we closed the place down.

"Top of the John," I ventured, trying to be witty.

"Top of the 'Cock," he fired back.

Five or six of us piled into his little Honda for the drive, and the sight of us—humanities graduate students at the University of Chicago, dressed in our only suits and ties, or dresses and heels—must have made passersby think of us as a circus act. I hardly recognized the girl I hadn't helped move in. She wore a purple, belted dress; her hair was beautifully done; and she had lipstick on. There wasn't room for all of us to have our own seat in the car, and so I sat in the front seat and she sat on my lap. I looked at her and thought (or may even have said aloud), "You really *are* pretty."

That winter, more snow fell in Chicago than anyone could recall. The streets remained unplowed, especially in Hyde Park (which had long been an "independent" ward and, therefore, got few city services). By January, we were walking from the dorm to campus over snowpack as high as the roofs of the parked cars, and every now and then, an antenna would poke through, or we'd scrape along a battered sunroof. We traveled in packs: ill-fitted students from the Midwest and the east coast, terrified of Hyde Park's reputation in the late 1970s, constantly looking over our shoulders even in daylight.

On Sundays we would sit in the dorm, eating take-out Chinese food or fried chicken, and I saw her, with her knife and fork, cutting up the chicken breasts that the rest of us were eating with our fingers. One Sunday, I went out to Ribs and Bibs, a few blocks from the dorm, with money from the group to buy a full-size bucket, and as I stood in line—smelling the hickory wood, the vinegar, the ketchup, watching how they stacked up pieces of white bread at the bucket's bottom, just to soak up all the grease, counting the chicken pieces tossed in with the tongs—a cop car screeched to a halt outside and two policemen threw themselves out, one of them reaching for his gun and the other yelling, "He's in Ribs and Bibs!" I threw a twenty on the counter, grabbed my bucket, and ran out the back. I wondered just who they were looking for—nobody in the line looked arrest-worthy, and by the prison tattoos on the guy who served the chicken, I figured he had done his time. Maybe someone was hiding in the kitchen. Maybe someone was in the closet. I ran all the way back to the dorm, puffing in the winter air, holding the hot bucket to my chest, until I blew into the building, ran to the kitchen, and broadcast, "Listen to this." After I told the story, there was silence, and one of the students said, "Maybe they were looking for you."

To be a student at Chicago in those years was to share in the myths of intellect. Giants had walked the earth—Robert Hutchins, Enrico Fermi, Harold Urey, Saul Bellow, Milton Friedman—and the English department prided itself on the legacy of the "Chicago Critics," a group of scholars who took shape in the decades around the Second World War and who formulated, more by accident than by design, a view of literature that stressed the formal understanding of the verbal work, the nature of genre, and a sense of literary understanding grounded largely in the *Poetics* of Aristotle. Most of the old Chicagoans were dead. Some of their students were professors in The Department. But there remained a group of grad students who'd stayed on, half-believing that Richard McKeon would come out of retirement and teach again, or that Norman Maclean would decamp from his Montana retreat and approve their half-finished theses. These were men in their forties who remembered long-retired faculty as vigorous professors, men who talked about Samuel Johnson's *Rasselas* as if it were the model for all prose fiction, men who believed that if you just read a book hard enough, if you just paid attention closely, if you just listened, then no critical response was even necessary.

At the beginning of my second year, I took my general exams. I put on a tie, walked into the examination room, and faced the three professors. They welcomed me, looked at my list, and then Wayne Booth—in a white turtleneck and blue blazer, with his deep white beard, looking like Moses in Johnny Carson's clothing—began: "Tell me about the final line of, oh, *Great Expectations*." And I parried, "I saw no shadow of another parting from her." And he said, OK, how about the last line of Hopkins's "The Windhover," and I replied, "Fall, gall themselves, and gash gold vermillion." For thirty minutes, he tried to trip me: Bellow's *Herzog*, the Middle English *Sawles Warde*, Otway's *Venice Preserved*. I'd managed, over the summer, to read so deeply and so passionately in all my books, paid close attention so hard, that I'd virtually memorized the texts. I don't think we discussed anything at that exam, but as the other examiners looked on, Professor Booth and I traded quotations until, after an hour or so, he asked how well did I know Chaucer's *Reeve's Tale*, and I said, "Better than my own Bar Mitzvah portion." And to please him, I recited the beginning:

> At Trumpyngtoun, nat fer from Cantebrigge,
> Ther gooth a brook, and over that a brigge,

And then I said, you see, it's all about that little river and the mill and how the narrative flows in the space of time, and there's the Thames, which Chaucer had to cross to get to Southwark and the Tabard Inn, and, of course, you know how the tale responds to the Miller's—a tale all about water, and the flood, and the fear of being drowned not just in life but in language—and then I said, "and the whole thing ends with a proverb":

> And therefor this proverbe is seyd ful sooth,
> 'Hym thar nat wene wel that yvele dooth.'
> A gylour shal hymself bigyled be.
> And God, that sitteth heighe in magestee,
> Save al this compaignye, grete and smale!
> Thus have I quyt the Millere in my tale.

And he said, more like Moses than like Johnny, "I don't think we need any more. It's traditional for the candidate to step out of the room for the committee to discuss his performance, but in this case I can tell you that you passed. Congratulations." And he stood up, pulled his notes together like he was gathering the tablets, and strode out of the room, leaving me and the other two examiners in mute amazement.

Terms passed. The girl I met the first day went to dinner with me, once and then again, and soon I was sitting in her room, watching *Saturday Night Live* on her black-and-white TV, leaving a clean pair of underwear in her drawer. Some time in winter quarter, Hans Küng disappeared from her bookshelf. In August, we moved in together.

I read furiously, took my seminars, and put together a hundred-and-forty-seven page dissertation on debate and dialogue in medieval poetry. Still riding on the fame of my oral, I convinced my examiners to pass the dissertation, got them to write letters for my applications, and two and a half years after entering the PhD program, I interviewed for and received a job offer at Princeton.

The Princeton English department at that time was run by a charismatic Arkansan who'd been an undergraduate at Princeton, went to Oxford on a Rhodes, and then came back to teach, get tenure, and chair the department like a small-town Southern mayor. He'd look at you and shake your hand and somehow drag your secrets out of you. He knew just who had slept with whom, who was repressed, and who was barely out. He loved to break careers, coddling fawning assistant professors right up to the vote against their tenure, and then apologizing—who knew this was coming? He announced, on the morning of my campus interview, "We tenured a woman last year," and it was unclear to me whether he was speaking out of pride or relief. He asked about my family, and I said, "My brother is a senior here." "Well. Oh, by the way, I won't be at your lecture," he announced, as if having a brother who was then a Princeton undergraduate was good enough for him, as if seeing that I wore a Brooks suit and a tie and a white shirt and polished wingtips and knew all about his own work (Are you still writing on Stevens? Isn't Miss Austen the most sublime of novelists? Joyce, of course, is inimitable,

I slavered) was the interview itself. Just before he left me in his office, he said, almost as an afterthought, "And what will Mrs. Lerer be doing here?"

And so I asked the pretty girl who sat on my lap in the car, who'd moved in with me and made puff pastry in our apartment kitchen, who'd studied French, who came to campus with a TV and high heels and ate take-out chicken with a knife and fork, who told me stories of her California family and their St. Louis ancestry, who let me know her uncle was the most important curator of American art in the country, who told me of her mother's spinster aunts who grew up next to T. S. Eliot, and whose father, a retired marine colonel, looked exactly, when I'd met him, like Robert Duvall in *The Great Santini*, to marry me.

We did the wedding by ourselves. We ordered all the food, commissioned engraved announcements, and secured the services of a university Unitarian minister who promised not to use the word "God" in the service. We invited twenty-four people: my parents and my brother, her parents and her uncle and his family, her sister and her brothers, her high school best friend, my grad school buddies, and my dissertation advisors. Dad and Mom were divorced by then, but they showed up with my brother and played the parents, Dad in a dark suit and floral tie, Mom in a pearl-gray skirt and matching silk blouse. Mid-April still was brisk in Chicago, and we stood outside Bond Chapel at the university, our breath white, mingling that Saturday morning, when my future in-laws came up. I introduced my parents and stood by, waiting for something magical to happen, as if Dad would charm them with his diction or Mom would say something adorable about me as a child, but before anything theatrical could transpire, the Great Santini grumbled, "It'll never work out." Why, Dad asked. "They're of different faiths."

The ceremony, the lunch, and the exchange of gifts passed without further words between the sets of parents. The museum curator uncle had brought cigars for us all, and the Great Santini (whom I remember chaining them, one off another, when I visited the family in California), took one, bit the end, and lit it up like he was smoking out an infestation. Dad, who had smoked for thirty years, declined, but Mom took one, poked a little hole in the end with her fork, and held it out for me to light it. She sat there with the cigar, letting it burn but not puffing, and looked at me as if to say, "Who am I doing?" and broke into an accented song:

> Falling in love again,
> Never wanted to.
> What am I to do?
> Can't help it.

Mom and Dad left on different planes. My in-laws disappeared after the lunch, and we were left with Uncle and his family. I don't remember how the afternoon passed, but by evening we were all together at the Moon Palace restaurant on Cermak, piling up moo shoo pork and Uncle talking about how we had to visit them—in New York, on Park Avenue where they had lived for twenty years, or in Connecticut, at the farm that his wife's family had owned since the 1750s. And I remembered, as he talked, what my wife had told me about him: that he had gone to Exeter and Harvard; that he'd found a wealthy Radcliffe girl and married her at nineteen; that his in-laws were descended from the most influential people in the country. I'd spent a day at Regenstein Library researching the two of them. Her father was the founding partner of a major New York law firm and the son of the president of Yale. Her mother was a society scion of a lumber baron and his Virginia Four-Hundred wife. He specialized in the paintings of the Hudson Valley School, and after a brief turn as curator at a museum in upstate New York, had secured a place at the Met, where he'd risen to chief curator of American art.

And I remembered, at that moment, that this very evening was the first night of Passover; that it had completely slipped my mind; that I had lost track of the Jewish year; and now, on my wedding night, was eating moo shoo pork with my new aunt- and uncle-in-law, thinking, I bet I'm the poorest Jew he's ever talked to.

One evening in the early 1980s, I found myself in a rented tux at their twenty-fifth wedding anniversary party. His wife's many cousins had assembled, along with his Harvard roommates, at a Manhattan club so exclusive that it prided itself on having spurned the current mayor of New York. I sat at a table next to the founding director of the largest optical firm in the world. His formal wear bristled with gold shirt studs, each in the form of a love knot, with matching cuff links and a large, gold love knot hanging from his watch chain. He showed up with a woman at least twenty years his junior, with hair dyed the color of his studs and enough jewelry to arm a battalion of escorts. At one point, somewhere between the tallowy lamb and the watery sorbet, a tall gentleman in his midseventies approached our table. His turnout was impeccable, the lapels just the right width, the peau-de-soie pumps just the right buff. Everyone at the table stopped their babbling, as his visit commanded an absolute respect. And when he came up to me personally, a shiver passed along the silverware. "May I have a word, young man?"

I got up, and we walked over to a sideboard. "I understand you teach at Princeton, is that so?" Yes, it is. "And am I correctly given to understand, as well, that you are something of a scholar of the classics, yes?" Yes. "Well, have you ever come across the work of Edward Kennard Rand?" Yes, sir, he was a professor at Harvard and one of the most important early twentieth-century figures in the study of late antiquity. He did the defining edition of Boethius's *Consolation of Philosophy*, on which I'm writing a book. You know, it's funny, but I've never heard anyone speak of . . .

"He was my undergraduate advisor."

And then he walked away, leaving me at the sideboard with my rented, plastic shirt studs and my unwritten book, watching him retake his seat at a table of his contemporaries like Jacob Marley dining with the dead.

The following morning, we assembled at the anniversary couple's apartment on Park Avenue for a midday meal with the visiting cousins. There, I learned that the gentleman who had approached me was a distant relative, a past president of the club, and a grandson of the former president of the New York Stock Exchange. As we assembled for drinks (this at eleven-thirty in the morning), I met relatives from the old St. Louis days, Hudson Valley squires, and my host's mother-in-law, who close up still had all the aura of the 1920s debutante she'd been and who, in conversation, sounded just like Katharine Hepburn. I sat next to her at the meal, and I looked down at the table setting as if it were on loan from the Metropolitan Museum's hall of armor. Three forks, arrayed by size, guarded the left side of the gold-rimmed china, while three knives stood at attention on the right. Above the plate sat two spoons, polished to a fineness that reflected my astonished face like a fun-house mirror. Goblets and glasses ranged across the table, and a woman in an apron and a doilied hat stood by the kitchen door. My head went back and forth, until it lodged before the silverware, and Uncle's mother-in-law put her hand on my shoulder and said, "Just go from the outside in, dear."

Four years later, we finally accepted her invitation to dine at her own house along the Hudson. My wife and I drove in to Manhattan from Princeton on I-95, through the bleak marshes of Elizabeth, through the Lincoln Tunnel, and then crosstown, up Third Avenue to catch the lights, and over Eighty-Eighth Street to Park. Our sad Tercel jostled among the Caddies and the BMWs, and I found a barely legal space between a hydrant and a loading zone. The doorman met us at the awning of Uncle's building and showed us to the elevator, and we went up. I remembered the apartment from the anniversary—dark, paneled, with a kitchen out of 1935 and a single, black rotary phone in the hallway. A large canvas from the nineteenth century hung in the living room. A bit of American primitivism, it showed unyoked oxen, woolly sheep, and gamboling deer around a riverbank. Under its gilt frame, far too ornate for the painting, was a metal label: *The Peaceable Kingdom.*

Uncle was in a foul mood. Having foolishly agreed to drive us all up to his mother-in-law's, he faced the prospect of two hours in a car too cramped for his self-esteem and was already anticipating my intrusive questions about family and work and paintings and all of the things that made them, to me, as exotic as the Mud Men of New Guinea. The last time I visited the Met, I told him as he filled a carton with the white wine we would drink at lunch, I went straight for the Michael Rockefeller room. Michael Rockefeller, I repeated. You know he disappeared while on an expedition to New Guinea. He loved to collect that crazy stuff. Those amazing wooden sculptures, with their big heads and sticklike limbs, had always captivated me. The body masks, the long boats, and the shields were fascinating in their fearfulness. Ranged on the white museum walls, they stood out like alien armor; as the sound of the drum came to me in my imagination, I could hear the Asmat warriors joust against the spirits. Was that the beat that Rockefeller heard as he fell from his canoe? Was his "desire to do something adventurous"—a phrase repeated in the museum's brochure—as much an escape from his own demons as into someone else's dreams? What do you think? Do you think they really ate him?

"We were at Harvard together," was all he said.

We piled into their station wagon for the drive upriver, leaving the tangle of traffic behind us, riding through Yonkers, White Plains, and Tarrytown, past Sleepy Hollow, Hawthorne, and Thornwood to Armonk. Washington Irving country, I remarked, but the name sank like a pebble in the well of his indifference. Tell me about Aunt Bertha, I provoked, thinking that stories of the old St. Louis glory might prompt him to reminiscence.

"Aunt Bertha. Knew T. S. Eliot. Never stopped talking. Died my junior year at Harvard."

And then six beats of nothing.

"My father died when I was four, and after my mother remarried and moved us to La Jolla, I couldn't have cared. I left La Jolla because there was no culture. Old ladies keeping books out of the library. Older men building collections of bad art. Hollywood screenwriters driving down for three-day drunks. Raymond Chandler lived there. Hated it. Used to tell stories about how he would go into the public library and ask for his own books, just to irritate the librarians. I'm sure I saw him once, getting into an argument with one of those old ladies. 'Oh, you're Raymond Chandler, the writer,' she said. 'I read one of your books when I was in the hospital last year.' And then Chandler says back , 'I hope it didn't make you worse.' And then she pulls herself up. 'I wanted to throw it across the room, it made me so mad. But I didn't. There was something about the writing.' That was the thing about La Jolla—every now and then there was something about the writing, but most of the time you just felt everyone was happier not noticing.

"My sister, your mother-in-law, had to leave school to support herself, but by the time I was a teenager my parents had recovered enough to send me to Exeter and Harvard. The La Jolla schools were rotten. My brother lived through it and managed to wind up at Stanford, but I got out. Another story that passed around was about neighbors of Chandler's sister-in-law. Seems there was a family from Kansas who moved to La Jolla and put their kids in the public school where they all got A's, even though they knew nothing and did no work. All the family talked about was how, before they came to California, the kids worked hard and got nowhere near A's.

"My stepfather's mother came from a family that had all gone to Exeter and Harvard, so they got me in. That was where I discovered art. Real American art. Not quilts or watercolors or those Shaker boxes, but great paintings. Back then, a professor would put a slide of a Frederick Church up on the screen and say, 'This is a candy box. This is what they liked in the nineteenth century.' 'Nineteenth-century' was the most pejorative term you could think of. Sure, for the most part, nineteenth-century American painting is a provincial art. It's a mixed bag. French impressionist art of the 1880s, for example, is simply superior. But I'm convinced that, at its best, American art has a beauty and emotive power that is very much its own."

I listened to a conversation that had soon become a lecture, and remembered many of his phrases from a *New York Times* interview he'd given just a couple of years before. "Curator of the Hour," it was titled, and it gave a story that, even in the confines of the car, he was unwilling to enhance. I waited, but he said nothing to texture the caricature of the *Times*:

An angular man with a chiseled face and silver at the edges of his short brown hair. Behind horn-rimmed glasses, his eyes are green and direct. He wears, characteristically, three-piece suits complete with watch-fob.

I waited for his explanation of his habit, for something behind the *Times*'s surprise that, no Eastern blueblood,

in fact, he was born in Colorado, the son of an Army officer, and raised in California — small-town California at that. He remembers, as a boy, being alive to all things visual.

He'd drifted slightly into the left lane, just as a semi slung along his blind spot and blasted out a *hoot* that sent him overcompensating to the shoulder. He recovered, got us back into the middle of the turnpike, and his mouth closed like the panel of a mailbox. I'd half hoped he would rehash that article—relive his triumph of rehanging the famous *Washington Crossing the Delaware*. At nine hundred pounds, according to the *Times*, "it needed special brackets to support it." Once it was up, he thought it slanted to one side, and sure enough, a careful measurement of the paining showed that

it was indeed a half inch lower on the right side. The painting was duly lowered and the errant bracket remounted. It seemed like quite an expense for half an inch that nobody else saw.

I waited, unrequited, for the story of how nobody had seen, as well, the value of the Twachtman that he compelled the museum to buy a dozen years before. As the *Times* told it, here was this "green" assistant curator, making his first pitch to the board, and asking them to buy a large landscape, *Arques-la-Battaile*, by the forgotten American impressionist, John Twachtman. It had, he'd told the reporter, "come right down the middle of the pike at me." The pitch was difficult, the painting odd, the board silent, the curator brand new. But that night, the director called to say the purchase had been approved. And he'd been proved right. The Twachtman, now, was esteemed as one of the great American landscapes.

The week before, I'd gone off to the Princeton Art Library to call up a reproduction of the painting, hoping for a point of conversation. It didn't seem like much to me. Some grasses crisscrossed in the foreground, while flat water stalled behind them; then a riverbank, and then a gray horizon. I thought of Michael Rockefeller on his river, swimming to the drum, the surface flecked with blood and broken spear tips. But there was nothing of that here: the color palette was washed out, as if Twachtman had drawn a sponge across the face of the water. What had the curator, as green as the river grasses, seen in it? What came right down the middle of the pike at him?

Taking the *Times* reporter on a tour, he stopped before the painting, now hung in a place of pride:

> *It is only here that he stops. All around him is the cacophony of last-minute pounding, drilling, winching. It is a noise level which will never be heard here again. But he stands quite still, staring at this painting, oblivious to all. "Listen to this painting," he says. "Listen to the silence."*

We drove in utter quiet for the next half hour. And I imagined him, listening for silence on a flattened canvas, no touch of lurid color to disturb the green he saw reflected in his green eyes, no drum, no song; a peaceable kingdom, clear water for a boy alive to all things in small-town California.

We pulled up to the door, and he slammed the gearshift into park. He opened the trunk and lifted out the carton of wine bottles like they were Howard Carter's treasure. The girl was at the door—the same one in the same apron and cap who had assisted at the anniversary lunch. His mother-in-law appeared from behind the library door, her eyes comically magnified by the large lenses of her post-cataract glasses. Within minutes we were in the kitchen, sitting at a little table, Uncle opening the wine, the girl fiddling with the range. The gas flame came on with a *whoop*, and soon the nook was filled with the competing smells of melting butter, canned fish, and hot cream. Working the pan with her right hand, she took two eggs out of the carton with her left, broke them over the pan and quickly shifted hands to whisk them in. The wine worked like a drug on him. His shoulders dropped, his belly afforded release, and a mask of pleasure fitted to his face. I tried it: sharp tints of gravel, just a touch of flower, and a puckered citrus edge. We sat. Linen napkins, repoussé silver, cut crystal. The girl pulled four pieces of toast out of the oven, cut them into diagonals, and placed two on each plate. She spooned the concoction from the pot on to the toast points: creamed canned salmon, thickened with egg. Bits of pink fish floated on the yellowed sauce. Blots of brown nutmeg stained the top. And the toast points sank in the afternoon like Michael Rockefeller's dugouts.

"I understand," his mother-in-law said, as I picked at my points, "that you like books. Why don't you find your way into the library and see what you turn up." She pronounced "library" with two syllables. By now, most of the wine was gone and I was not alone in leaving an unfinished lunch plate, so I got up and walked through the hallway to the largest room I could find filled with books. It was a quiet space, well lit, facing the parkland to the rear of the house. It had jasper-green walls and embossed white figures on the wainscoting. At first, I thought it looked like Wedgwood, but then I realized that it looked exactly like the room in Kubrick's *2001*, where Keir Dullea, now prematurely old, sits in his dressing gown to have his food. I couldn't tell, at first, in what order the books were shelved, but then saw that they were ordered by their size: large folios flat on the bottom, then the quartos, octavos, and duodecimos. Not all were old, but none looked read. I took down a blue-bound copy of *The Education of Henry Adams*, to find Henry Stimson's bookplate on the inside cover: Stimson, secretary of war to two presidents, Hoover's secretary of state, supervised production of the bomb. There was a story around Princeton, told by the remaining Oppenheimer cronies, that Stimson crossed off Kyoto as a target because he remembered the city from his honeymoon (the bomb went, instead, to Nagasaki). I opened another, a late eighteenth-century Cicero, and found here the bookplate of Elias Boudinot.

That fall, I had been named the Elias Boudinot Bicentennial Preceptor at Princeton. An honor reserved, so they told me, for the junior faculty they hoped to tenure, the preceptorship gave assistant professors an extra year's leave, a research account, and a title. When I received the letter telling me about the award, I flipped to the back pages of the *Princeton Register* to see its history.

In memory of Elias Boudinot, president of the Continental Congress, and Trustee, 1772–1821

1950–1951	A. Warren, Jr., English
1954–1954	A. Warren, Jr., English
1958–1961	A. A. Sicroff, Modern Languages
1961–1964	C. F. Brown, Comparative Literature
1967–1970	O. R. Young, Politics
1970–1973	S. Molloy, Romance Languages and Literatures
1973–1976	S. A. Barnett, Anthropology

I knew *S. Lerer, English,* would go underneath, along with the dates, 1984–1987. The year I got it, I would read myself to sleep over the *Princeton Register,* scanning the lists of everyone who had ever had a preceptorship, imagining my name among those of my senior colleagues and the well-known dead, then turning pages to read off the lists of chaired professors, reaching back to the mid-nineteenth century, and imagining myself among them.

Elias Boudinot. Like Henry Stimson, he had been a distant relative of my host. I reached for another book, by Boudinot himself: *The Age of Revelation.* Foxed page after page of turbid prose fell through my fingers. Instead of reading it, I smelled it, and it had that rich, dark smell of leather, damp, with insect leavings. I sat in one of the stuffed chairs and turned the pages, scanning, first, for anything of interest, then, as I tired, for my own name. A hundred pages in, I found it: "the children of Seth distinguished from the children of Cain, by the appellation of the sons of God." I looked for the word "Jew" and found it: "the Jew for his darling partiality to his own nation and ceremonial law." I sat there like an adolescent with his first unabridged dictionary, looking for the dirty words, just to see them in print to prove that they exist. I looked for the word "love":

> *. . . and to the studious, contemplative philosopher, who, pursuing the plastic hand of nature through all the streams of pure benevolence and love, hath been led, with astonishment and surprise, to the inexhaustible ocean there . . .*

I fell asleep but did not dream. The book slipped from my hand, dropped on the floor, and woke me up. My wife came in and said that it was time to go, the afternoon was at an end, and our host had to take her nap. I put the book back, almost telling her of my discovery, but held my tongue. We all drove back to Manhattan in silence, down the Hudson, with the Sunday traffic streaming back into the city, our windows up against the exhaust fumes.

EIGHT

Kaddish

I woke up in Dad's apartment, holding the pictures from my wedding. The week's rain had tapered off, and I got up and went into his bathroom to throw water on my face before the drive back down the peninsula. The bathroom was as old and as original as the apartment's kitchen: checkerboard tiles, old double faucets, the H and the C worn down to shadows on the white enamel handles. As if to brighten it all up, he'd hung an oversize poster of Marilyn Monroe over the toilet. It showed only her face, the outlines merely suggested in black, but the lips full, deep red, and barely parted. I turned my back to it and washed my face, half expecting it to disappear when I reopened my eyes. But there it was, filling the mirror as I raised my head, her lips the only color in the room.

The week after he died passed like someone else's play. I must have slept and eaten, hugged my son and kissed my wife, but nothing stayed with me. I canceled one class but returned for the next to find my students ranged around the table, each with a card and an embrace. One of the students presented me with an over-large bouquet of flowers. Her mother was from the island of St. Lucia, and she often came to class in Caribbean floral prints. That day, she'd broken off one of the blooms in the bouquet and put it in her hair behind her ear. And as she greeted me, her eyes filled with tears, she was as beautiful as if she'd been one of Miranda's daughters on that dark island.

I don't remember what we talked about that day. I do remember that I let them all write final papers on topics of their own choosing—just make sure you use the theoretical materials we read in class, and locate your analyses in the broader arc of the key themes of the course: memory and authority, citation and quotation, gender and interpretation, signification and commodity. For the remaining weeks, we met to discuss their projects; I read rough drafts, held extended office hours. When they came in, it was like transcriptions of telepathy. Each student knew just what to say to prick my attention. One wrote about Poe's "Purloined Letter" and the hunt for meaning. Another wrote about the Russian poems she had listened to in childhood, read by émigré parents. Another noted that the first words she had ever written, as a five-year-old, were "cat, dog, zoo," and then she spun out a reflection on how these three words encompassed all of literary understanding, binaries of cats and dogs, literary history as a zoo, each author caged for our amusement. The student with the flowers wrote about Agatha Christie's *Body in the Library* and Virginia Woolf: how women shape narratives out of household life, how class and culture mattered to the English, how the reader is a body in the library.

Were they so brilliant that they intuited all my interests? Or was I so transparent that every class became an essay in self-understanding? Were they out to please me, or to get the grade? Was there anything more than duty in those flowers? *Poor man*, I thought, *my library was dukedom large enough*.

By the end of the term, I'd called the friends, ordered the food, and set the date for the memorial at our home in Los Altos. We pulled down everything on the living room walls and put up his pictures, and as guests arrived I pointed out Larry in all his different roles. Here's the photograph at four, in the Buster Brown haircut and short pants. Here's the Bar Mitzvah portrait, in his yarmulke and tallis. Here are the wedding pictures—look how skinny he is, and look how radiant Mom is. Here are the pictures from his plays: Dracula, the Impresario, the Pasha, Tubal. And over here, the head-shot he commissioned when he moved to San Francisco, looking for a part. Finally, on the table by the guest book, there's the last photograph. I don't know who took it, but he's sitting in a nut-brown leather jacket, mouth half-open, as if trapped in midspell.

Forty people came, many of whom I had never seen before. There were his friends from San Francisco, each accompanied by a woman just for the occasion (this is, after all, the suburbs, my wife had said). Some students from the fifties showed up. One of them, now the film producer I had heard so much about, showed up in a lemon-yellow rented Mustang and a six-day beard. Another of them had been one of my first babysitters. A couple who had worked the summer camps with Mom and Dad came, too. And his hairdresser, who had retired to Florida, had flown in on the red-eye just for this event.

And Mom. There she was, in pearl-gray slacks and a silk blouse, shaking hands and hugging people she had not seen in forty years. She was gracious to all the men, smiled at their escorts, and played with her eleven-year-old grandson on the carpet. She had already met my colleague, the Shakespearean, years before I presented Dad to him, and I asked him to the ceremony, thinking he would understand. His boyfriend had died just a few months before, and he was lonely, listless, underweight. My mother found him.

"Oh, my dear, it's so good to see you."

"Hello, Renée."

"Seth tells me you've had your own loss. I'm so sorry. How are you holding up?"

"I'm all right. You know, things are hard."

"Yes, I know. *Azoy geht es.* Or, as you would have said on the Upper East Side, *c'est la vie.*"

And then she popped a crab cake in her mouth and found her seat.

I'd pieced together a memorial out of prayers I found in books on Jewish mourning. I built a library of sorrow on my desktop and planned a service based on prayers I'd never heard him say. I blessed him in a language he would barely have commanded. One of my guidebooks limned a service for me, defining the loved one's passing in "a final breath" and stressing that Jewish law encouraged "brevity in funerals." I wanted it as short as he would have liked it. High Holidays came back to me. We would sit on the benches and before the rabbi even started, flip to the end of the section in the prayer book, calculating just how long we would have to spend in temple. Passover Seders bubbled up, as we'd speed through the Haggadah before the roasted chicken. The book I liked best was encouraging: a service should be just "a chance to say some words." But brevity was not finality: "Jews continue to talk with the dead."

That must be why I became a college professor, I said at the ceremony. For many years, I told his friends, I've been a scholar of the past. I've written books about medieval and Renaissance literature, about legacies of academic life, about the histories of words and their pronunciation. Most recently, I've focused on the history of childhood. Children have learned how to read and write by memorizing alphabets, by imitating sounds and letter forms, by attending to great initials in their Bibles or their Psalters or their history books. Children and literacy come together, as boys and girls learn to read not just books but people, things, experience. A child, wrote one seventeenth-century churchman, "is a man in small letter," and "his father hath writ him as his own little story."

I was my father's little letter (I continued), and I tried to learn his language and his stories. At night, he would tell me fairy tales: "Rumplestiltskin," "Ali Baba and the Forty Thieves." Like all great fairy tales, they were about discovery, remembering, and forgetting. How often in nightmares we sit down to tests having not studied, or forget our lines as the curtain opens. Children's stories, much like childhood itself, brim with neglected tasks, lost talismans, long-faded rituals; with characters who can't remember, who misstep in their roles or forget who they are. *Never forget*. Children's books teach an art of memory by illustrating figures of its failure.

I gave my eulogy more as a lecture than a lament. The teacher in me came out, and I pulled out lesson notes.

When I was four (I said), Dad would lull me to sleep with "Rumplestiltskin." Each night he would begin with the fair miller's daughter who could, so her father bragged, spin straw into gold. He would tell me how the king heard about her gift, and how he coerced her into spinning for him. One night, as she sat fearful of being found out, a little man appeared out of nowhere. He spun the straw into gold for her and, as repayment, asked for her necklace; the next night for her ring; the third night for her firstborn child. She agreed, and the king soon married her. Years later, when her son was born, the little man came to claim his due. This time he made another deal with the distraught queen: if she could guess his name, he would relent. She made guesses, and so did we.

Each night, Dad and I would go through scores of names, from the familiar to the mad: Charles, James, John; then names of friends and relatives—Sam, Sid, Norman, Sy; and then the Yiddish names, like incantations from a distant magic—Chaim, Lebbel, Mendel, Menasha, Velvel. The queen kept guessing, too, and eventually she sent a messenger in search of the little man. This messenger came upon a campfire with a ring of little men.

And in the middle, in the very fire, was the imp, dancing and singing, "Rumplestiltskin is my name!" So, when the little man came
back and asked, "What's my name?" the queen said, "Rumplestiltskin." And he stamped his foot so hard he drove it into the
ground, and then he picked himself up by his other leg and tore
himself in half.

This was my favorite bedtime story, I went on, and as I tell it
to you now, I know I was his firstborn and that he was so afraid
of losing me, and I was so afraid of losing him, and so, in the
bedroom that I soon would share with my new, baby brother, we
would sing our songs and play with names.

And at that moment, though I had said nothing, I knew why
my brother was not there, why he refused to share in Larry's
ceremony, why Dad had favored me. I broke the tension and my
own regret by saying that it was traditional, as I understood things,
for family and friends to say a few words about the deceased, and
if anyone wished to speak, we'd all be glad to hear it.

Right away, the man who showed up in the lemon-yellow
Mustang, the producer who was once, nearly fifty years before,
a student in his ninth-grade class, stood up.

"The thing that I remember about Larry is his socks. The first
day of ninth grade he showed up—the teacher, in a corduroy suit
and a bow tie and these purple socks. Who wore purple socks?
I'll never forget it. He stood up and he told us he was going to
teach us something about English literature whether we liked it or
not. I don't remember a thing he said. But I'll never forget those
socks. Larry was great. Even when I was working in Hollywood,
I always made time for him. Let him use my place in LA, the one
in Bolinas, too. It's funny, he always used to think I'd get him into
pictures. I loved him like a father, but he was no actor."

Another man stood up, a member of the same ninth-grade class,
the man who was my babysitter the year I was born.

"I'll never forget the day Larry took me for my driving test.

My dad had a Plymouth Ventura, and it was a pouring rainstorm, and you know in those days they tested you on the hand signals. Even if the car had directionals, you had to stick your hand out to signal left, and then do this bent thing with your elbow if you were going right, and then the opposite way if you were going to stop. So there we were, lining up in the car for the test. I was eighteen, and Larry was sitting in the passenger seat having a cigarette, like we were going to a movie. It was my turn, and I pulled up to the white line and began. It was pouring rain, and I had to have the window open the whole way to do the hand signals. By the time I'd done half the course, I was soaked, and by the time the test was over there was a little puddle down by the pedals. I passed, and Larry was great; we went out for an egg cream afterward at Garfield's. Years later, when he went into the hospital for his hernia operation, I felt I had to pay him back, so I drove him to the hospital that morning.

"Seth, you'll remember the day we went out in the boat. You couldn't have been more than six, and Larry and I and my niece, who was about your age, all drove down to the harbor in Canarsie, and we rented a little motor boat. I don't know what Larry had in mind, but I remember the guy at the rental dock looking very funny at us—two guys, two kids. We got in, and I remember how you sat up at the prow and liked to feel the spray on your face. Larry pulled the throttle out full, and we sped along, past tugboats and sailboats, and then he cut around to bring us back and he probably lost control, and we wound up stuck on a sandbar near the shore. The outboard motor had stalled out, and the propeller was jammed in the sand. And Larry took off his mocs and rolled up his pants and got in the water, it was up to his knees, and he squished through the sand to try to get the propeller unstuck. He pushed and the boat moved a little, and he stood back and said, fire it up. So I pulled the cord and the motor started, and I turned the lever to engage the prop and the thing just whined and spun and jerked up out of the sand and flipped itself up on the balance bearing of the engine mount. There was this propeller in the air, spinning and spitting water and sand, and there was Larry, covered in crap."

I remembered that day, just as he had. I remembered, I added too, the year that Larry was commuting between Cambridge and Brooklyn, and on weekends we'd go back to that marina in Canarsie and go out on the party fishing boats. We found an old guy, Captain Jack, which I doubt was his real name, and he'd take us out with a bunch of old men. The first time we went out, Dad and I got so seasick we couldn't even fish. But he insisted we go out again, and a couple of weeks later we did and I caught a big black bass — as Dad lay in the hold looking green. I remember Mom cleaned and cooked that fish and it was great. The next week, we drove down to Captain Jack's, and he was there with a group of older men I'd never seen before. They were standing around, smoking, and I remember Jack coming up to Dad saying, look I can't take the boy out today. You, fine, but not the boy. It's, well, it's too rough.

And then I looked at Mom and risked it. Of course (I said), my mother always thought that Captain Jack was running drugs or guns, or doing something for the mob, and to this day she believes that that morning he was going out beyond the twelve-mile limit to drop off a body in the sea, or meet a Cuban boat.

She laughed, and I knew I had her.

Would anyone else like to speak?

The hairdresser who had flown in from Florida stood up, just to say that Larry meant the world to him, that they were friends for twenty-five years, and that the best piece of advice he'd ever heard came from Larry: just do what's right for you. A married couple who'd come in from New York recalled how Larry and

Renée were such great friends at camp, and, "Renée, remember the camp sing?"—at which point, he broke into "Harvest Moon," but with rewritten lyrics about everyone at camp.

No one who knew him only from San Francisco spoke. Two Turkish brothers stood in the back. One was the man I remembered from the apartment, in his crisply pressed striped shirt, with his carefully trimmed gray hair. The other, over six feet tall, came in a leather jacket, with a mustache and goatee and slicked-back black hair. Khan. That was his name. He'd introduced himself as Khan. No subject, no verb. Khan.

They said nothing during the afternoon.

I stood there, thinking about Larry's socks and driving in the rain, and boats, and camp theatricals, and "Harvest Moon." And then *The Tempest* came back to me:

> *Down with the topmast! Yare! Lower, lower! Bring her to try with main-course. A plague upon this howling! They are louder than the weather or our office.*

Just do what's right for you.

> *If you can command these elements to silence . . . use your authority.*

I lifted up a prayerbook, then, and Hebrew spilled from me like spells. *Yitgadal v'yitkadash sh'mei raba. Yizkor elohim nishmat Leb ben Noah sh'halach l'olamo.* I said that, in traditional Judaism, you would tear your clothes, or a part of them, to expose the heart and signify a fissure in the family. "Jacob rent his clothes, put sackcloth on his loins, and observed mourning for his son many days." But now, we do it symbolically. And I picked up a remnant from his closet, a small piece of flannel that must have been left after he'd had a pair of trousers altered, and I held it up and said the prayer and ripped it so forcefully that flecks of wool flew off and mingled with the dust against the sunlight.

> *Graves at my command*
> *Have walked their sleepers, oped, and let 'em forth*
> *By my so potent art.*

And with the service done, I clapped my hands together and invited everyone to eat out on the patio, and Mom stood up and kissed me and said, "I guess I was just tired of playing the beard." And my eleven-year-old son, ill at ease throughout the afternoon, suddenly quieted.

NINE

Lithium Dreams

He had always been antsy child, ill suited for the classroom chair or dinner table. Dad doted on him, though, expecting him to love him for his gifts: enormous model airplanes, giant Lego sets, illustrated books on dinosaurs and fish and the elements. We tried to take him to a baseball game once, but we had to leave before the seventh-inning stretch, the boy bored and overheated. Instead of stories about sportsmen, we read tales of chemical discovery or strange facts about metals. He loved the Dorling Kindersley books, with their full-color pictures of mineral specimens and the men who founded science. Shortly before Dad died, I'd bought him John Emsley's *Nature's Building Blocks: An A–Z Guide to the Elements*, and we would sit up nights, A now being for Astatine, and B for Boron. We'd read about the rare earths, and names as unpronounceable as sauropods hovered in the air as he sank into sleep: Praseodymium, Dysprosium, Rhenium, Ytterbium. Some nights, we'd speculate on all of the unnamed, coded elements beyond those that had been firmly found: Unununium (111), Ununbium (112), Ununquadium (114).

One weekend afternoon shortly before Dad died, he got it in his head to start extracting all the elements. Some we would find; some we would pull out of machinery and products; some we would isolate from chemicals. "Lithium batteries!" he announced after lunch, and so, like knights on an adventure, we drove off to True Value Hardware to buy a handful of batteries, intent on opening them up. Outside, we set up carefully: rubber gloves, respirators, newspaper on the ground. Because of lithium's re-activity, I suggested we cover everything in Vaseline—a process that left us, begloved and masked, looking like two proctologists on holiday. We used a hacksaw to cut into the batteries, a move that released toxic smells and smoke. We spread apart the metal casing, resecting the elemental heart of the anode, and there it was: a coil of silvery-bluish lithium foil. We quickly covered it in Vaseline, put the whole mess into a jelly jar, and kept it, displayed like a captured creature, on the windowsill.

As we cut into the battery, I saw us both as surgeons of our adolescence, getting at the heart of something volatile. For as a child, I knew I had a lithium imagination. My oldest memories are not of events but of dreams: tongues of fire licking up around my bed, each one with a laughing face; my best friend's mother morphed into a monster; hallways, staircases, and elevators go-ing dark and nowhere. One day—it must have been when I was four—I came home after playing cowboys and Indians and, still wearing the headdress I had fashioned out of newspaper, I ran into the apartment, breaking something along the way. "My God," my mother screamed, "you *are* an Indian"—the first words I re-member her saying to me.

I looked down at the boy, benignly playing with his grand-mother at Dad's ceremony, fingering the bit of ripped cloth I had held up with my prayers. I remembered, how, soon after my brother was born, I went into my mother's dresser, pulled out one of her white sweaters, and cut holes in it with a scissors—as if to show her how the fabric of my own life had been torn. If I could tell you of my childhood, I thought, would it make yours better? *'Tis time,* I recalled Prospero,

I should inform thee farther. Lend thy hand,
And pluck my magic garment from me.

Like, you, I was intractable. I spent the bulk of kindergarten in the corner, crying "I'll be good" to a teacher so old and so ugly I was sure she had a tail. When we did homonyms in second grade, I proudly stood up for my own, and offered, in my Brooklyn English, "orphan" and "often." I was sent to the vice principal. The Brooklyn of the early 1960s was a place where children played outside, where you could ride your bike all day as long as you were home for dinner, and where you could stand on a street corner waiting for adults to come by. "Would you cross me, sir?" I was taught to ask, and unsuspecting children of my generation gratefully took strangers' hands and walked across the street. On such streets, I was menacing. Stickballs would carom over windshields; mothers would come out of doors to curse us out in Yiddish. When I was six, I found a fiver in my pocket (perhaps it had been given to me by my grandmother), and I waltzed into Phil's corner store with my friends and ordered up a whole mess of pretzels and red licorice, each piece, a penny. "What are you doing with that five-dollar bill?" Phil chastised me. "Now, you go home and give that right back to your mother."

As if to pay me back for my six years of Indian exuberance, Mom put me into therapy. Each Wednesday afternoon, she would take me in a taxi to 39 Park Street to see Dr. Lisbeth Sachs. She had a vaguely European accent, which in those days was a mark of medical authority, and we'd sit there for an hour, talking about dreams, or having tea, or making things with popsicle sticks. One day, after my mother gave the cabbie the address, he turned around and said, "Lot of doctors on that street, eh?" "Just mind your own business," my mother snapped back (with, of course, the implied "goddamned" hovering between "own" and "business"). I never really got much out of these appearances, save when my mother would herself come in, and Dr. Sachs would ask some piercing question and Mom would break down in tears.

We all went on drugs. Mom lived on Milltown and Librium for

the better part of the Kennedy administration, and while Jackie's pillbox hats absorbed a nation, Mom's pillboxes spilled over the kitchen table. I was given Thorazine, much stronger than the sedatives Mom took. Thorazine is now one of those relic drugs out of the age of thalidomide and lobotomies, something that, I am told, they no longer prescribe even for homicidal schizophrenics. Whole stretches of my childhood have evaporated from me; I have no memory of third grade. When people of my generation sit down and recall where they were when John Kennedy was shot, I say nothing—if only I could shoot back that I was so medicated that I could barely dress myself, as if my 1963 had been assassinated by a pill. When I recounted this experience to a psychoanalyst in Palo Alto and asked him if they still used Thorazine anywhere, he said, "Oh, probably in some prison in Mississippi."

In the Mississippi of my childhood, I took refuge in the things of nature. There was a book in the Time-Life Nature series that had pictures of all of the elements, with evocative descriptions and arresting chapter titles—I remember one, "A Deceptive Façade of Solidity," a phrase that, in retrospect, could well have stood as an epigraph for my entire family. Weekends, we trooped off to the American Museum of Natural History, with its minerals and meteors. I memorized all that I could, and began to collect whatever elemental objects I could find. From there, I moved on to rocks and gems, once forcing my father to accompany me to some ancient jeweler's hovel on Canal Street to beg for samples. Crystals and cut stones arrested me. Light seemed to disappear inside them, only to emerge more brilliant and more colorful than when it entered. I would spend hours staring at the Star of India in the museum's Morgan Hall, watching how the asterism moved as I moved, wondering whether the faint star was really there or was just a trick of light. There was, at the museum too, an emerald crystal the size of a fist and a topaz larger than a suitcase. At home, I built my own collection out of jewelers' chips and castoffs.

We went to the New York World's Fair in 1964, where I spent an entire day at the Brazil pavilion, gawking at amethysts and geodes. I bought a few broken pieces of citrine, of smoky quartz, and of amethyst there (probably for no more than fifty cents), and thirty-five years later, when I learned to facet gemstones, these were the first pieces I cut.

But the most beautiful of all were tourmalines; rich reds, dark greens, fluorescent purples. My favorites were the watermelon tourmalines, crystals that moved from green to white to pink, as if they were plugs cut from some stony, seedless fruit. They were like candy, and I soon learned that their many colors came from lithium. Lost in the silicate, trace metals made them beautiful. What trace metals could enter me? Was there some strange impurity that would enable me to trap the light, to make it shimmer as it left, to help me move from rind to sugary inside?

The word "lithium" comes from the Greek *lithos*, meaning stone, and for the early nineteenth-century chemists who found it—and its elemental peers—it must have seemed almost magical to conjure little blobs of metal from these rocks. Men such as Sir Humphry Davy, or Johan Arfvedson, Jöns Berzelius, or Robert Bunsen would place the rocks in acid, leach out the metallic salts, and then recover them as crystals. They heated these compounds to what must then have been unheard-of temperatures (common table salt, for example, melts at a temperature greater than copper, silver, or gold) and ran electric currents through the melt. God knows how they got their electricity. I imagine great banks of wet batteries, slabs of copper and zinc in jars of acids, bubbling away and putting out raw voltage that would split these compounds into elements. And at the anode, there would be a little gleam: lithium, sodium, potassium, calcium. Chemistry was more than a science; it was theater, and seeing the results of such electrical and coal-fueled power must have been like watching Vulcan walk out of the forge with gleaming steels.

Remember (I would turn to him) how much you loved *Uncle Tungsten*, the memoir by Oliver Sacks? That's where we read how Humphry Davy isolated alkalis and how, as a young boy, Sacks took great pleasure in repeating Davy's old experiments. He would take bits and pieces of the metals and throw them in water, watching them sputter and burn. Once, he writes, he secured a three-pound chunk of sodium solely for the purpose of tossing it into a nearby river and creating an explosion. "This," he writes, "was chemistry with a vengeance."

Sacks had as much of a "chemical boyhood" as we did: the fascinations with the elements; the love of organizing life into clear categories; the power of chemical reactions. And yet, he had a childhood ripped from home. Sent off to boarding school in 1939, he found a break from all the bullying and terror of the classroom in observing nature. The winter was "exceptionally cold," with "long glittering icicles hanging from the eaves of the church. These snowy scenes, and sometimes fantastic snow and ice forms, conveyed me in imagination to Lapland or Fairyland." He goes on:

> It was during the same winter that I remember finding the window-panes of the rectory doors covered with hoarfrost, and being fascinated by the needles and crystalline forms in this, and how I could melt some of the frost with my breath and make a little peephole. One of my teachers — her name was Barbara Lines — saw my absorption and showed me the snow crystals under a pocket lens. No two were ever quite the same, she told me, and the sense of how much variation was possible within a basic hexagonal format was a revelation to me.

We read this passage one night, and when you are older I will tell you how it called to mind so many other versions of the story. One day, I'll read to you from Adalbert Stifter's *Indian Summer*, a lovely nineteenth-century story of a young boy's fascination with the plants and animals, the rocks and minerals of nature. Like us, he built collections ("Since childhood I had tried to get many a sample for my collection") and saw landscapes in the frames and fissures of crystals. When he climbs the Alps and looks out on their frosty peaks, he recalls what it was like to look out of frozen windows:

> When moisture in the form of tiny droplets that can be scarcely seen even with a magnifying glass comes onto our window panes from the vapor in the air, and the necessary cold temperature also sets in, then the whole sheet of lines, stars, fans, palms, and blossoms that we call frosted windows is created. All these things come together as a whole, and the rays, valleys, ridges, and knots of ice are wondrous to behold when examined through a magnifying glass.

Like looking at snowflakes under a magnifying glass, Stifter subjects bits and pieces of the child's life to close scrutiny. The brilliance of Sacks's similar reminiscence lies in its filtering through this device: as if the magnifiers of his memory were not the facts of life but the tropes of fiction.

My Dr. Sachs had no such insight, but when she would say things like "Your dreams are windows to your psyche," with her rich rolled *r*'s like Viennese whipped cream, we believed her. I think I always trusted people with an accent: something authentic about it, something that took us back to the deep past of our European roots. Maybe that's why so many Americans love Oliver Sacks, with his perfect English colored only by those slightly "wabbit" *r*'s. Maybe, too, that is why you find the books of W. B. Sebald on my nightstand. His characters are displaced and disturbed; but so, it seems, was he. "Memory's Einstein," Susan Sontag christened him, as if to evoke not just the obvious association with the genius of relativity but, more subtly, to make Sebald—with his wiry gray hair, rich mustache, and émigré's affect—the accented authority of our time.

In Sebald's *Austerlitz*, the hero of the novel recalls how, as a young boy in the 1930s, he was sent off from Europe to England on the *Kindertransport*; how he lived with a Welsh couple; how he attended a boarding school; and how he forgot his name and language. One day, "during the coldest winter in human memory," he returns from that school to his adoptive family in Wales, where the mother is dying:

> There was a coal fire smoldering on the hearth of her sickroom. The yellowish smoke that rose from the glowing coals and never entirely dispersed up the chimney mingled with the smell of carbolic pervading the whole house. I stood for hours at the window, studying the wonderful formations of icy mountain ranges two or three inches high formed above the crossbars by water running down the panes.

This scene recalls precisely Stifter's prose. It also recalls a moment earlier in Sebald's novel, when his narrator visits the eye doctor. Something has impaired his vision, and one gray winter day he takes the train to London to visit a Harley Street specialist. Sitting in the overheated waiting room, the narrator anticipates the angst of Austerlitz in the death chamber of his Welsh adoptive mother:

> From the gray sky that lowered over the city outside a few isolated snowflakes were floating down, and disappeared into the dark chasms of the yards behind the building. I thought of the onset of winter in the mountains, the complete absence of sound, and my childhood wish for everything to be snowed over, the whole village and the valley all the way to the mountain peaks, and how I used to imagine

what it would be like when we thawed out again and emerged from the ice in the spring.

Artistic memory replaces lived experience: as if the only way to grasp the glitter of our childhood or face our fears in doctors' offices is to retreat into allusion. Childhood gets filtered through the snow of books. The white page and its letters look for all the world like snowy streets. Our schools are filled with Mrs. Lineses, showing us all how to lineate our lives. And in our coldest winters, we seek to be transported out of our rooms.

My parents must have hoped that we could transport ourselves out of our city rooms, but little changed after we followed Dad to Harvard. We lived on quiet streets, with lawns and lots. I visited the Peabody Museum, whose collections lay in dusty cabinets, the minerals and cut stones lying on their sides, the old handwritten labels foxed and curling up around them. I dragged my parents off to quarries, where we'd pick around the tailings looking for crystals in the dross.

I fell in with a friend whose father was an optical engineer for Itek, one of the many research firms that sprouted around Boston's Route 128 in the 1960s. He'd bring home electronic gear from work and set up strobes and lasers in his basement. One day we developed a project to photograph a drop of milk. My friend, his father, and I took a thin aluminum pie pan and attached a wire to the rim. We ran this to a battery and then to a strobe light. The connection then ran to a strip of metal that we placed underneath the pan, so close as to be just not quite touching. We filled the pan with milk so that the bottom of the pie pan bowed within a millimeter of the metal strip. We turned off all the lights, and opened the shutter of a camera focused on the pan. Standing on a ladder, I held a medicine dropper full of milk. I let a large drop come down, and as it plopped into the pan, the bottom bent just enough to complete the circuit, fire the strobe light, and catch the splash of milk in the fractional second of its flash. The open camera captured it, and when we had the film developed we could see the crown of flying milk, the big bulge in the middle of the circle, and the smaller droplets flying out like jewels in a tiara.

We sent away for model rockets, and on winter days in Massachusetts we would trudge out to snow-covered fields and set up launching pads. Each rocket came with a self-contained engine, a firing device, and a parachute designed to deploy at the top of the arc of flight. I had my friend take a picture of me standing next to our creation, and I posed like Robert Goddard posed in the famous photograph, taken in a Massachusetts winter in 1926, just before he launched the first liquid-fueled rocket. Like Goddard's, our rockets often crashed and burned. Most times, the parachute would fail to open, or would partially deploy, only to flail as a burning plastic streamer behind the cardboard and balsa rocket body as it plunged back to the field. Only once did our parachute open, and then the wind caught it, blowing the rocket a quarter mile away into a stand of trees. We stood there, helpless but happy that the thing had worked, and yet we never would recover it. And I imagined what it would be like in the spring, when the snow thawed and the trees bloomed and someone would stop by and see this strange fruit hanging beside hemlocks.

One winter later we were gone. The basement in the Pittsburgh house became my lab. There I assembled retorts and reagents to extract radioactive elements from my rock collection. I ground up bits of pitchblende and mixed them with acids, generating brilliant green solutions that fluoresced under my ultraviolet light. I laid specks of my distillates on paper-wrapped sheets of photographic film. After they were developed, the films showed stray black marks, exposures from the radioactivity. I broke up handfuls of thermometers to collect blobs of mercury. And I read deeply in the "Amateur Scientist" column of *Scientific American*, trying in vain to follow their instructions for such things as a magnetic resonance spectrometer and a Van de Graaff generator.

About the only bit of equipment I mastered was a cloud chamber: a pickle jar, the cover lined with black velvet, a bit of alcohol dripped in, and the whole thing inverted onto a block of dry ice. With the lights out and a flashlight beam set tangent to the jar, we saw the fronds of vapor trails left by stray particles as they passed through the alcohol-infused air, ionizing as they went.

Twenty years later, in the fall of 1986, I fell apart. Days passed and I could not get out of bed. I didn't shave for a week. At the time I told myself it was the stress of coming up for tenure, or the tensions of five years of marriage. I lay in bed, replaying my interview with the department chair, remembering how he would coddle his assistant professors into complacency, only to let them drop. I thought about that afternoon upriver, in the library with Elias Boudinot's books, steeling myself for the humiliation of losing my job. And what would Dad say: we don't think he'll get it. What would he think if I turned out to be what one of my predecessors had been: a brilliant junior medievalist who, two years after being denied tenure, was found by a senior professor selling ties at Brooks Brothers in Manhattan.

I'd given up my lab for the library. All of the things I'd hope to do in childhood, the person I had wanted to grow up to be—all that was over. At thirty-one, I had accomplished only one thing in my life: to stay in college and wear tweeds. I lived in the afterglow of Dad's Harvard afternoon, when men who'd known Henry Adams tottered up to ask directions. I thought of Grendel groaning, of my Iceland summer. I thought, if I just got dressed I would feel better. And then I recalled the story of my predecessor selling ties.

My bedside books that autumn were the ones I'd taken from Dad's study. There was Maynard Mack's *Modern Poetry*, still with the Barron's Textbook Exchange slip inside it. And there was F. O. Matthiessen's *Oxford Book of American Verse*, with a few dog-eared pages in the Frost section. I split the book open at "My November Guest":

My sorrow, when she's here with me,
Thinks these dark days of autumn rain,
Are beautiful as days can be;
She loves the bare, the withered tree;
She walks the sodden pasture lane.

I got up and called the hospital. Give me a pill, find me a solvent for this sorrow. They referred me to a psychiatric pharmacologist, a man my own age, confident, well-spoken. Why are you here, how do you feel, is this a sadness or a true depression?

Her pleasure will not let me stay.
She talks and I am fain to list:
She's glad the birds are gone away . . .

Count backward from one hundred by sevens, he instructed. Ninety-three, eighty-six, seventy-nine, seventy-two. I spit the numbers out without reflection. The doctor said, "Red boat, blue boat, green boat," and then he asked me to repeat the sequence. He asked me about my weight, if I was regular, if I had ever done the stamp test (you take a roll of stamps and adhere them around your penis at night, and if the roll has broken in the morning, you know you've had a night erection and you're not impotent). He asked me, once again, to list the boats in the same order that he'd said them.

Red boat, blue boat, green boat.

"Let's go with lithium," he said.

I picked up the prescription at the hospital and swallowed. Within days, I felt my fingers twitch, my memories blur. The final lines began to disappear, and as I prepared for my classes, I was terrified that I would forget something. Weekly, I would show up at the clinic just to see if the titration levels were correct: too much lithium, and I would fade; too little, and I'd sorrow. After a month, a mineral crust covered me. I carried Dad's anthology around, my finger stuck in "My November Guest." I'd wander around Princeton, poking into Einstein's yard or loitering in the physics building. Some afternoons, I'd walk the mile or so to the Institute for Advanced Study.

The desolate, deserted trees,
The faded earth, the heavy sky, . . .

Thirty years before, J. Robert Oppenheimer ran the place. The director's house still had the white corral that Oppenheimer had put in for his young daughter's horse—an animal that, Princeton legend had it, she fed chocolate milk out of a porcelain teacup while her parents argued in their alcohol-fueled anger.

Before the coming of the snow . . .

Oppenheimer's ghost still walked those lanes, arguing over policy or protons, still locked with Edward Teller over what they called the "super."

Teller's hydrogen bomb would never have been built without lithium. For what he realized (or what he would always take credit for realizing) was that in order to get hydrogen atoms to fuse and thus release the massive energies of thermonuclear explosion, you had to use the element's heavier isotopes. Deuterium and tritium would fuse, theoretically, at lower temperatures than simple hydrogen. So, on an afternoon somewhere in the Pacific, in the year before my birth, Teller and his minions supervised the wrapping of a regular, atomic bomb in a casing of lithium deuteride. This compound, when exposed to the immense heat of the atomic blast and the release of radiation, would do two things: first, it would transmute the lithium into tritium; second, it would fuse the tritium and the deuterium in the compound together. It worked.

She's glad the birds are gone away . . .

I walked the sodden Princeton streets, remembering the duck and cover drills of elementary school, the fallout shelter in the basement of the fire station, the doomsday clock twitching to midnight. I remembered the terrifying television ad for Johnson's presidential campaign — the little girl, the flower, and the countdown. *Ten, nine, eight* . . . and then the blast. I took my lithium, walked through the Institute, and waited for the end. It never came. I got my tenure that spring, with a phone call from the chair, who said, in one breath, "Congratulations. Don't disappoint us." I went into the bathroom, opened up the bottle full of lithium and dumped it in the toilet. It didn't spatter like the metal, didn't flame out colorfully. It just dissolved.

"I guess I was just tired of playing the beard."

And with Mom's kiss, the funeral was over. I smiled and looked at you, and thought how blessed you are that, with a California childhood, there would be no frosted windows to get in the way; how you would always be our prince; and how your only lithium would be in batteries.

TEN

Beauty and the Beast

Years passed after the funeral. We settled Dad's estate, sold off his things, and took the pictures down. I taught my classes, wrote my books, and watched our son's chemical imagination blossom. He built a laboratory in the garage, stocked with chemicals I helped him purchase off the Internet. He put together equipment for pyrotechnic displays, thermite reactions, electric dazzlements. I raided the old physics laboratory at Stanford just as they were moving out: Tesla coils lay in dumpsters; piles of diffraction gratings sat outside offices, waiting to be trashed; lenses and light boxes spread themselves across floors, like Prospero's detritus. I thought—I can control this beast, I can tame his impulse to explode. When friends visited, we would sit in the backyard, and after barbecue and biscuits, he would come out, like a showman, and turn an upended trash can into his podium. He'd place a little powder on a plate and drop some liquid glycerin on it. Smoke would appear, and then a lilac flame. He'd take a handful of steel wool, an ordinary battery, and some wires and burn it up before our eyes. He'd throw some chemicals on to the still hot barbecue, and flames would spectrum out: strontium carmine, lithium red, copper green, sodium yellow. And for his final act, he would ignite some powdered metals on the trash-can lid. Blinded into bliss, we applauded every trick behind his chemical theater.

But howsoe'er you have
Been jostled from your senses, know for certain
That I am Prospero.

The garage was his court, and his teenage attendants waited on him as he lectured on reactions and reagents. One afternoon, he brought a friend home from tenth grade, a fellow member of the science bowl team. He pressed the button on the garage, and as the door rose he stood there, arms thrown wide out, and announced, "This is it."

Pray you look in.

School fell apart. We had him tested. "But he's brilliant," I would protest, as if simply loving him would make him work, as if my desire was enough to bring him to my fold. I would come home from teaching or the library and smell the weed on him. I'd drop him off at playgrounds where he used to ride the swing and watch him meet his buddies, young men now, with their first beards shadowing their smiles. His government I cast upon my wife, *and to my state grew stranger . . .*

And my trust,
Like a good parent, did beget of him
A falsehood in its contrary as great
As my trust was . . .

Finally, after stabs at therapies and private school, we realized that we'd have to have him taken from us, "involuntarily transported" to a place to get him clean, to keep him safe, to teach him how to be. Like Caliban in exile, I thought, thrown out of his bed. I'd wake up in the middle of the night and walk in his room where he would sleep, encircled in his sins.

this thing of darkness I
Acknowledge mine.

We had him taken just before he turned eighteen. Faced with his erratic behavior and the threat of an arrest record, my wife and I met with an educational consultant and together planned his transport. This woman, in her seventies, spoke to us in a blend of care and pity. She would make the calls, arrange the transportation, and make sure that when he arrived at the euphemistically named assessment facility in Utah, all would be in order. We sat there in her office, and I thought of Dr. Sachs. I half-expected that she'd lead me to a little room and we'd make popsicle-stick houses together, and she'd remind me that our dreams are windows to our souls. But she gave us the names, and one night in early April my wife and I drove to a motel outside the Oakland airport and met with the two moonlighting cops who would take him. They explained to us the procedure: they had done this many times; just be prepared for his attempt to bolt. I let them know that he slept with his pocket-knives next to the bed, and they said, "Get them out." They helped us script this dreaded night: they would arrive at 5 a.m. We'd say good-bye, tell him we loved him, and then leave the house. If all went well, he'd be at the facility in rural Utah by dinnertime.

He fell asleep in a bedroom still filled with picture books. There was *Goodnight Moon,* with its litany of the green room, the pictures on the wall, and the bunny. There was *Pat the Bunny,* its fur mottled by years of stroking. There was *Carl's Masquerade,* his favorite at three: a picture book with no words, with the Mom and Dad dressing up for a costume party and the baby left in the care of the dog, Carl. See how the baby rides Carl to the party, I remembered saying to him. Nobody recognizes them, because they think they are in costume, too, and there are Mom and Dad, Mom beautiful as a princess and Dad dashing as a pirate, and the baby and Carl win the prize for the best costumes at the party, and then they go home, just in time to be in bed when Mom and Dad return.

What costume would he wear now?

They came, as planned, at 5 a.m. We woke him up. We sat there in his bedroom, telling him we cared, telling him how it was all for the best. And then we left and sat in the car a block away, watching them bring him into their car, watching them drive off, knowing that soon they would be in an airplane en route to the Utah desert.

After we had him taken, I went through his lab. There were shrink-wrapped containers of compounds I knew we hadn't bought together: reagents for drugs, a setup for chilling the heated mixture. There was a stash of marijuana and some pills I dared not recognize. I thought of how I'd done this all before, how I'd rifled through Dad's closet only to find things that made me wonder: did I know you? I sat there on the concrete floor of the garage, surrounded by substances, and wished Dad back, less to ask for advice than for approval. I thought of Sebald's stories of the *Kindertransport*, little children taken from their homes and set on railroads to supposed safety. And in my thoughts, I rewrote passages from *Austerlitz* to match his days: *I thought of the onset of winter in the mountains where we'd sent him, the complete absence of sound from him, and my childhood wish for everything to be snowed over,* the garage, and the lab, and the late nights, and the slammed doors, and I imagined what it would be like when we would thaw out, when we would speak again and I would tell him of my father, and of how he'd read me "Rumplestiltskin," "Ali Baba," "Beauty and the Beast," and we would remember that the bedtime stories all resolved to happy ends.

In "Beauty and the Beast," a merchant, having lost his fortune, seeks news of his ships. He travels far from home, leaving his daughters, and gets lost in a forest. He takes refuge in a castle, is treated to great hospitality by a mysteriously absent lord, and then meets that lord—the Beast—when he plucks a rose to take home to his daughter, Beauty. In compensation, the Beast must have Beauty with him. She comes, and he treats her with great elegance and courtesy. He makes her promise never to leave him, but when she begs for a week's leave to visit her poor father, he agrees. "Do not forget your promise." But she does, overstaying her time at home. Almost too late, she remembers, and she has a vision of the Beast dying in his garden. "Forgetting all his ugliness," the story goes, she throws herself upon him. "You forgot your promise," Beast replies. But Beauty, moved by the inner nobility of the Beast, pledges herself to him as his wife. With this, the Beast is magically transformed into a handsome prince, released from a spell cast by a wicked fairy.

The story worked a magic on me as a child, a magic that materialized one evening, at fourteen, when my parents and I saw Jean Cocteau's film *La belle et la bête* at the Carnegie Library in Pittsburgh. The library was running a historical film series, and it was Mom's idea to go. She wanted to see something in black and white. And it was beautiful: Jean Marais with his shoulder-length blond hair, Josette Day looking like a porcelain goddess, and the Beast with eyes like hot coals. People slipped in and out of walls, arms stuck out holding candelabras. At the end, Marais, as Avenant, the human suitor of La Belle and a crony of her brother, goes after the riches of the Beast's Temple to Diana. He has the magic key to let him in, but he opts instead to break through the temple's glass skylight. *Du verre, c'est du verre,* glass is glass, he says, as he pushes his foot through. And yet, it is not, for in fairyland the glass is always something else: a mirror is a portal to a hidden world, or a deceptively transparent barrier between reality and fantasy. When he breaks the glass and tries to get in, Diana shoots him and he is transformed into the Beast. At that precise moment, the Beast rises before La Belle and we see him as

Prince Charmant, played by the same actor who played Avenant, Jean Marais. *Ou est ma bête?* "Where is my Beast?" says Beauty. He's gone, and the prince explains: my parents never believed in fairies, so the fairies punished them through me.

Du verre, c'est du verre. We'd led a mirrored life. Mom sits forever at the vanity before her wedding. Dad leaves me at the airport with the broken glass beneath the car door. When memories come back to you, it says in *Austerlitz*, "you sometimes feel as if you were looking at the past through a glass mountain." *Du verre, c'est du verre.* I look through the glass and see the forks and knives that seemed to come alive. I slip through doorways to forgotten libraries. I see all the books I've read and written about, trying to imagine myself in them. Like Alice, I go back to get the little golden key. Like Scrooge, I want to go back to school. "You recollect the way," says the spirit. "Remember it!" Scrooge cries, "I could walk it blindfold." And yet, when he visits Christmas Yet to Come, he sees himself forgotten by all but the gravestone.

Where is my Beast? Where is my Wonderland? Let me remember their lessons. If you hold the strangely written "Jabberwocky" to a glass, "the words will all go the right way again." And when the White King shouts out that his terrifying moments are ones he will never forget, his Queen notes, condescendingly: "You will though, if you don't make a memorandum of it." But when the King begins to write, furiously, in his memorandum book, the pencil is too thick for him. "I can't manage this one bit. It writes all manner of things that I don't intend." The pencil always was too thick for me. As a child, I scrawled, I blotted. My beautiful words showed up on the page as beastly scribbles.

If only I could make the words all go the right way again.

Let me rewrite his childhood. Let me start again with all his books. Let me read *Winnie the Pooh* to him and explain the words. Let me teach him. Let me explain how Pooh's line about living "under the name of Sanders" is a joke: he literally lives under a sign with that name on it, but it's an everyday expression to say that someone is living under another name. Let me explain TRESSPASSERS W, the broken sign whose erstwhile threat of prosecution Piglet turns into an identity. It is, he says, short for his grandfather's name, Trespassers Will, which in turn was short for Trespassers William. And at the story's end, when everyone is ready for a party, the gifts given are the tools of writing:

> It was a Special Pencil Case. There were pencils in it marked "B" for Bear, and pencils marked "HB" for Helping Bear, and pencils marked "BB" for Brave Bear. There was a knife for sharpening the pencils, and India-rubber for rubbing out anything which you had spelt wrong, and a ruler for ruling lines for the words to walk on, and inches marked on the ruler in case you wanted to know how many inches anything was, and Blue Pencils and Red Pencils and Green Pencils for saying special things in blue and red and green.

Now let me tell my son that we can start to write. "Was Pooh's pencil case any better than mine?" Christopher Robin asks, and the father-narrator replies, "It was just about the same." A man, I'd like to say to him, in my best professorial voice, should be measured by the quality of his pencil case.

I've measured out my life against my pencil case. I've found books in which I could underline myself. That afternoon in Armonk, as I looked for anchorage in an old widow's library, I thought of Henry Adams, finding himself in his father's bookshelves. I remembered how I had studied for my orals, how I knew just how every work of literature had ended, how I'd parried with Wayne Booth as he thrust and feinted with quotations. In what books, now, will I find my solace?

I hold Sebald's *Austerlitz* in my hands, the underlinings from ten years ago unfaded like the outlines of a face. It is the story of a man ripped from his childhood, who has lost his name, and who returns to his home city. Like Scrooge, he walks the streets again as if blindfolded. He finds records of his parents: a flamboyant father and an actress mother, one who had starred in operettas, who had taken him to her performances, who dressed him up, at times as a player in a fairy tale of her own imagining. The photo on the book's cover depicts a little boy clad in white, with a furred cape, breeches, and a huge plumed hat; when Austerlitz finds his aged nursemaid still alive in Prague, she shows him the picture and tells him the story, six decades old. His mother "had the snow-white costume made for you especially for the occasion. On the back it says, *Jacquot Austerlitz, páže ruzové králnovy,* in your grandfather's handwriting." Jacques Austerlitz, page to the Rose Queen. Or better, Jean Marais in Cocteau's film, rising up off the ground with his elaborate plumes and dazzlingly white cloak. There is a prince in all of us, as long as we believe in fairy tales.

Have I stopped? My son always had troubles with his memory. He would forget to brush his teeth, stumble over assignments, fail to recall basic math facts, or sit quietly, lost in a dream world, while the rest of us remembered our chores. He never wrote well. The pencil would slip from his hand, the point would break. I could never read his homework.

At the facility in Utah, he was obliged to write letters home. The staff would take his angry, scrawled pages and scan them into PDF files, send them to us, and await replies. I'd pore over his penmanship, digitally remade on my screen. I'd try to get past all of his forgetting—how he wouldn't own up to his habits, how he led us astray, how he would deny and dispute everything he was accused of doing, and just why he was out in the mountains in the first place.

Where was the prince I played with? When I dropped him at the schoolyard, in those evenings after high school, would he transform into a beast? When he went out on his own, friends with cars picking him up, should I have expected him to come home changed, blood between his teeth and sweat streaming?

In his first letter home, my son asked for one book: Jules Verne's *Mysterious Island*. I knew immediately why. It is a story of a group of Union prisoners who escape a Confederate camp toward the close of the Civil War. They build a balloon and set off, but the wind blows them off course and they wind up on an uncharted island where they have to rebuild civilization itself. They mine saltpeter for gunpowder, smelt ore, fire pottery, even create the instruments for electricity. When a shipment of equipment washes up on shore, they cannibalize it for both needs and luxuries. And when, in the end, Captain Nemo makes his return appearance, they realize that they were not alone—that all this time, they were under knowing eyes. I believed when I received his letter that I must have taught him something—that if he were going to find his way back, it would be through a book.

He took that book with him, eight weeks later, when he went off to wilderness therapy. From northern Utah, with its mountains and its June snows, we drove him six hours south, into the Red Rock canyon lands, and dropped him off in hundred-degree heat. For three months, he would live with a group of boys in desert sands, hiking unblazed trails, cooking for himself, and sleeping without tents or tarpaulins. He had a pack, a bedroll, and a book, and midway through his journey, we drove out to visit him. The therapist assigned to him met us in a small town near the Arizona border, and we drove ninety minutes into nowhere. And there, stopping by a landmark I could never find again, he was. He'd grown a frazzled beard, his hair was long, and he was brown with sun and dirt. When I collected rocks and minerals, I'd look for stones that had been blown by wind and sand so that they had a natural shine. Desert polish, I called it. That's what came to mind when I saw him, and we sat together, his mother and I, his therapist and him, and we talked about how he'd learned to wipe his bottom with live leaves, how he chewed on the juniper and wildflowers, how the team left jugs of water at each campsite, but how he had also learned to forage for refreshment. One day, he told us proudly, he ate nothing but crickets. And then he took out a ziplock bag of seeds and raisins, and he offered some to me and to his mother, and he said, "This is lunch."

I thought: this is his Iceland, this his time alone, the solitary sky spread out above him like a bedsheet for his dreams. I thought: and let me tell you of my own time, walking across rivers to bring fish for dinner, herding cows, living amid a language not my own. Let me tell you about the sheep-head dinners and the blood-pudding, and the day the relatives came and they bought a tomato. Let me tell you all of this, as we sit here in the dirt, eating your seeds.

But I did not. I sat there thinking only of the move that we would make when we returned: from Palo Alto to La Jolla, a move that had been in the works for over a year but that we'd planned to finalize that fall. I'd wanted so much to be solicited, so much to have an island of my own, a dukedom large enough. My Stanford classes had grown smaller in the years since Dad had died. The course I had been teaching that fall never regained its popularity. Enrollments fell away. I found my undergraduates more focused on their résumés than on the reading. No more Mirandas filled the rooms.

And so, when a deanship opened up at the University of California at San Diego, I applied. In the interviews and recruiting visits I bragged about how I knew the area, how I'd been visiting since the late 1970s when I first met my future in-laws, and how much my wife was hoping to move home. I varnished stories of my mother-in-law's family, of Sunday dinners on Mount Soledad, of how she had graduated from La Jolla High School before going off for one aborted year at Pomona College, of how her

marine husband brought the family back to San Diego County
to serve at Camp Pendleton. I told them how my wife had been
the valedictorian of Carlsbad High School, of how she'd gone on
to college at Berkeley, of how we truly cared about the University
of California.

My future colleagues enticed me with stories of the founding of the campus. A former military installation, it became the
seedbed for Roger Revelle's idea of a university. Émigré physicists
would share space with composers; oceanographers would find
solace at the Playhouse. I listened as men who had smoked with
Oppenheimer at Los Alamos assured me of their love of Mozart.
They told me of Revelle's accomplishments: how he discovered
in the chemistry of seawater the proof of global warming; how
he imagined modern universities as the equivalent of medieval
cathedrals.

And they assured me that the place was safe, now. My in-laws'
La Jolla was long gone, shattered when Revelle broke its restric-
tive covenant. "You can't have a university," he said in tones that
ultimately cost him the first chancellorship of the campus, "without having Jewish professors. The Real Estate Broker's Association and their supporters in La Jolla had to make up their minds
whether they wanted a university or an anti-Semitic covenant.
You couldn't have both."

La Jolla got its Jews and its university, and I got the job.

In the fall of 2010, my wife moved to La Jolla with me, and
we moved our son into an independent living program in Los
Angeles. We would drive the hundred miles each month to see
him, to convince ourselves that we were doing right, that he was
well. But the outcome was mixed, and by the summer he was in
another house in LA.

Last chance, I thought.

That summer, I would drive up on my own on weekends, take

him out to dinner, and watch him order in a restaurant, eat platters of salads and onion rings, and every now and then, share a dessert with me. Saturday afternoons, we'd wander into bookstores, and I'd watch as he selected Moleskin notebooks for his jottings, handbooks for his hobbies, or a novel of adventure.

> *Thou didst smile,*
> *Infused with a fortitude from heaven,*
> *When I have decked the sea with drops full salt,*
> *Under my burden groaned, which raised in me*
> *An undergoing stomach to bear up*
> *Against what should ensue.*

———————

As his time away drew to a close, we met one evening at Skylight Books in Los Angeles for a reading by my former student. She had been a member of that class the day my father died, nearly eight years before. She was the one who wrote about her first story, "cat, dog, zoo," and she had graduated, done an MFA, and published her first novel. There she was in a bookstore surrounded by her family and friends, a girl I still remembered as nineteen, incongruous to me in lipstick and a floral dress, reading from her novel about a young girl in a dystopian future. America has been shattered by an ecological disaster, and a generation has decamped to an offshore island where everything comes from the sea and where dim memories of cities hover in their heads like myths. The mother of the teenage heroine is missing, and as the book begins the girl is fingering a silver charm, a family heirloom of a forgotten world:

> The charm was silver, a small scaly bullet-shape that her mother had explained was called a pinecone. . . . Darcy had imagined pinecones

were fruit and wondered what they tasted like. The charm itself tasted familiar and foreign, like Darcy's own teeth and like some far-off salty earth, and sucking on it gave her a furtive, inward pleasure.

She read, and my son, now nineteen himself, looked at her like an oracle, as if to say, "You know, I've actually eaten pinecones." We bought the book for him and he devoured it in a day. It was, he told me later, like living in the wilderness.

I had believed in books. And I believed in fairies. I'd hoped that, one day, he would emerge off the ground, like Jean Marais, in cap and cape, leaving the beast behind. *Trespassers will be prosecuted.* But now, there is no one left to do the prosecuting. The imagination, be it the Hundred Acre Wood or Wonderland or the Beast's castle, never, in the end, truly prosecutes its trespassers. Everyone gets a second chance. And so have we. I have not been admitted to his secret places, but I think I'd rather find us welcomed there than in the countless classrooms of our back-to-school nights, looking out of windows onto playgrounds, or across glass partitions of probation. *Du verre, ce n'est pas du verre.*

After sixteen months away, our son is back with us now. Like Shakespeare's Puritan successors, we have shuttered up the playhouse of his passion. My wife and I moved out of the old house, boxed his lab away, and put his childhood books back on the shelves. Our tempest cooled, he sleeps not as a monster but a man. My wife cooks simple meals, and we sit down together, dinners shorn of drama. And Prospero, entering in act 4, turns to the son he never had, and asks forgiveness:

If I have too austerely punished you,
Your compensation makes amends, for I
Have given you here a third of mine own life.

The Soldier's Tale

In the spring of 2011, I was approached with an idea. A cellist in the Music Department thought that it would be great fun to put on Igor Stravinsky's *The Soldier's Tale* and have me play a part. It would, he promised, fill the hall. After all, he said, how many times does someone get to see a dean onstage?

In preparation, I spent weeks listening to the piece on YouTube. *The Soldier's Tale* recounts the story of an infantryman who makes a deal with the devil, trading his treasured violin for a book that, it turns out, lists future values in the stock market. In the course of the performance, he dies and returns to his hometown, only to discover that no one can see him. Eventually, he tricks the devil into playing him at cards, wins back his violin, and beats the devil into dancing. The props call for a fiddle and a book of spells, but there are no directions about stage sets or costumes. There is no singing; the actors read their lines in set pieces, interlarded with musical vignettes played by a chamber orchestra.

Originally, the cellist had thought of casting me as the devil, but he changed his mind when a retired faculty member—a performance artist, now nearly eighty, who had shared in some of the original Happenings of the 1960s and had lost none of her girlish narcissism—all but insisted on performing. The chance to cast her as the devil was too tempting for him, and so I was reassigned the soldier's part.

We spent days trying to rehearse. The artist could barely come in on cue and spent most of our rehearsal time trying out dance moves that her body now could only hint at. The narrator was played by a British art historian, chosen for his plummy accent and his height, though he found it too difficult to speak in rhythm with the music and, eventually, stopped coming to rehearsals all together. But I was there for all of them: on time, on point, on book.

The day before the scheduled performance, I went out on my own to buy some props and costumes for the show. I drove into Oceanside to find the largest Army Navy Surplus store in Southern California. Nestled between the marine base and the water, Oceanside was as busy with military as it had been thirty years before, when I accompanied my father-in-law to get some hardware for a home repair project. Just like that day, I walked the streets in a button-down shirt and loafers, threading through the crowds of overly tall twenty-year-old boys and their even younger wives, the only man with a beard in a sea of shaved heads. I found the Army Navy store and walked along its aisles, pulling down a camouflage shirt and a matching cap, grabbing a bullet belt, and picking up out of a bin marked "Five Bucks Your Pick" a discarded gas mask. I went up to the counter, spreading my haul before the cashier like Viking booty, when a young man threw the front door open so hard that it banged against the wall. He must have been six-six, blocking the California sunlight with his shoulders, booming.

"I just got back from a year in Afghanistan. Some son of a bitch stole my bedroll. I need another one."

And as if I had vanished from the counter, the cashier left me, strode down one of the aisles and picked up a new bedroll for the returning soldier. Ringing it up without even noticing me, she called the soldier "hon" and told him she'd knock off half the price, just for him. He stood there, all bald head and bicep, and looked down at my camo shirt and cap and belt and gas mask and said, more in confusion than in sneer, "You going to war, buddy?"

No, I said. I'm in a play.

The next night, we went on. The hall, in fact, was full, and even though we had had only one complete rehearsal, everyone felt confident that it would be a great success. I stood at the back of the theater in the shadows, wearing my camouflage cap and shirt and carrying a backpack with the soldier's fiddle in it. I hung the gas mask around my neck and waited for the music. It started, and the British art historian—who had shown up five minutes before the performance, in a tuxedo—read his lines impeccably, and I trudged through the audience as heads turned and a few people clapped. I walked up on the stage and opened my mouth to speak, and with the first word out there was a loud twang. We all turned to find that a string had broken on the bass fiddle. The conductor stopped the performance right there, and the bassist went offstage to change the string. We would begin again.

I stood there, my mouth still half open, not sure if I should remain in character, wearing my camo cap and thinking, no one will ever take me seriously after this.

After what seemed two phases of the moon, the bassist returned and we began again.

I read my lines, the artist came on, mincing in leotards with a butterfly net, turning an allegory of World War I into a hippie happening. Nothing went wrong after that point; we hit our cues. The lines we read, in the version of Michael Flanders, sounded more like Dr. Seuss than Stravinsky, but as we came to the end and the musicians played the closing chorale, I read to the audience's silence:

No one can have it all,
That is forbidden.
You must learn to choose between.

One happy thing is every happy thing:
Two, as if they had never been.

We each successively walked offstage, the narrator, the artist, and me, and as the last notes ended the audience stood up, applauding loudly our audacity, and we came back onstage and took our bows, and then, backstage, I greeted everyone—students and colleagues, old couples who had no other place to go, people half-expecting me to be in makeup, and a woman who broke through the crowd carrying a copy of a book I had written, saying she had only that day heard that I would be in the performance and, please, would I autograph it. She gave me the book, and I told her how touched I was that she had come. I took off the camouflage cap and took up her pen, and resting the book against her back, I signed my name.

I had a little nut tree, nothing would it bear,
But a silver nutmeg, and a golden pear.

I kept two items from Dad's closet: the nut-brown leather jacket and a silver tie. Two weeks after he died, I put them on, and my wife and I went into San Francisco to the Castro Theater. *Mildred Pierce* was showing, and it was one of those nights when moviegoers at the Castro were expected to dress up in period costume. The line tailed down the block—women with hair in snoods, lipstick as red as Christmas, and the men in soft fedoras, wide lapels, and two-tone shoes. We stood in line, the late-November chill frosting our breaths, and someone looked at me, looked right through to the jacket and the tie, knew them as he had known his own palm, opened his lips and closed them, silently, only the white air coming from his mouth.

ACKNOWLEDGMENTS

This book began in autobiographical essays originally published in the *Southwest Review* and the *Yale Review*. I am indebted to Willard Spiegelman, editor of the *Southwest Review*, who supported my first efforts, graciously offering advice and encouragement. Sections from chapter 4 appeared as "My Mother, the Ingénue" in *Southwest Review* 91 (2006): 349-58. A much earlier version of chapter 9 appeared in *Southwest Review* 93 (2008): 531-42. I am grateful to J. D. McClatchy and the staff of the *Yale Review* for their commitment to my earliest essays on children's literature and for their expert editing of my writing. A few sentences in chapter 10 are adapted from "Children's Literature and the Art of Forgetting," *Yale Review* 92 (July 2004): 33-49. An earlier version of the prologue appeared in *Yale Review* 98 (October 2010): 39-48.

In addition to revising these earlier materials, I have adapted a few sentences in chapter 6 from my *Inventing English: A Portable History of the Language* (New York: Columbia University Press, 2007), and a few sentences in chapter 9 from my *Children's Literature: A Reader's History, from Aesop to Harry Potter* (Chicago: University of Chicago Press, 2008). The quotation from the novel in chapter 10 comes from Anna North, *America Pacifica* (New York: Reagan Arthur Books, 2011). All quotations from *The Tempest* are from the edition of Stephen Orgel (Oxford: Oxford University Press, 1987).

As this book evolved, I took guidance from many friends and colleagues. Jennifer Crewe and John Kulka brought their editorial experience to early drafts. Sarah Shun-Lien Bynum taught me about narrative pacing. Anna North helped me find the dramatic arc to my story. Joseph Dane knew what to keep and what to cut out. Kathryn Temple shared with me her own experience of writing personal, creative nonfiction. Denise Gigante has been an ardent supporter. Deanne Williams thoughtfully read many drafts and has worked rewardingly with me on reading, teaching, and writing about Shakespeare.

This book would not have seen its publication without the inspiring support of Randy Petilos of the University of Chicago Press. The editor for my *Children's Literature*, he welcomed the idea of this book from the start, and he has been a true partner in this project. Alan Thomas of the Press expertly shepherded my manuscript through the review process, and I am grateful to him and to the two anonymous referees who approached this unusual submission with attentiveness, care, and critical acumen that helped immeasurably in my revisions.

In his book *The Great War and Modern Memory*, Paul Fussell quotes Wright Morris as saying, "Anything processed by memory is fiction." I have not willfully manipulated fact here. But this is how I remember things.